T0114243

Confucius from the Heart

CONFUCIUS *from the* HEART

Professor Yu Dan

Translated by Esther Tyldesley

ATRIA BOOKS
New York London Toronto Sydney

ATRIA BOOKS
A Division of Simon & Schuster, Inc.
1230 Avenue of the Americas
New York, NY 10020

Translation by Esther Tyldesley

Translation rights arranged with Zhonghua Book Company through Macmillan Publishers Ltd., Toby Eady Associates Ltd., and Simon & Schuster, Inc.
Originally published in China in 2006 as *Professor Yu Dan Explains the Analects of Confucius* by Zhonghua Book Company, Beijing.

Illustrations by Chen Chuanxi

First Atria Books hardcover edition October 2009

Designed by Dana Sloan

Manufactured in the United States of America

10 9 8 7 6 5 4 3 2 1

Library of Congress Control Number: 2009013766

ISBN 978-1-4165-9657-8

CONTENTS

EDITOR'S NOTE

During China's week-long national holiday in the fall of 2006, CCTV, the state-owned national network that broadcasts throughout the entire country of 1.4 billion people, aired a seven-day series of lectures on the teachings of Confucius by a relatively unknown professor at Beijing Normal University named Yu Dan. No one, including Ms. Yu and the TV program director, expected these lectures on the centuries-old teachings would take the nation by storm. And yet, literally overnight Yu Dan became a media sensation and household name in China as the script of the lectures was soon compiled into a book titled *Yu Dan's Reflections on the Analects*. In less than a year the book sold an unparalleled 10 million copies, including some 6 million pirated editions.

A philosopher and educator, Confucius laid out social, political, and cultural principles that became deeply embedded in Chinese tradition more than 2,500 years ago. The *Analects*, compiled by his disciples long after his death, contains his main doctrines with their emphasis on personal and state morality, righteousness in social relationships, justice, and sincerity. And yet despite its noble status, Confucian doctrine was in and out of fashion throughout China's dynastic and modern eras. It was revered by a long line of emperors and rulers, for instance, in the prosperous Han Dynasty (206 B.C.–220 A.D.) and in the last century by the Nationalist leader Chiang Kai-shek, and despised by others, such as Qin Shihuang, the first emperor who unified China and founded the Qin Dynasty in 221, and most recently by the radical Communist leaders during the infamous Cultural Revolution (1966–1976), when Confucianism was debunked for its allegedly "feudal" characteristics that inhibited the country from moving ahead.

Moving ahead was all China did. Beginning in 1978 under the economic reforms inaugurated by Deng Xiaoping, the country's then paramount and pragmatic leader, China embarked on an unprecedented transformation in its economic and social life, achieving stunning economic growth and putting the nation back on the center of the world stage, both politically and financially. And China did this not so much with the aid of Confucian wisdom, but rather by borrowing from the capitalist model that was diametrically opposed to the "revolutionary" doctrines that had dominated the Chinese psyche since the coming to power of Mao Zedong in 1949.

This economic miracle, however, also brought unwanted changes and side effects that the Chinese people have often found hard to adjust and cope with, as the era when reading Chairman Mao's *Little Red Book* as a daily ritual and perhaps somewhat as a source of spiritual engagement is gone. Today, such rigid Communist preaching can no longer play this vital role. Chinese traditional religious life has not fully blossomed in the post-Mao era. The Christian Bible has only made its way through underground churches. Deng Xiaoping's famous catchphrase "getting rich is glorious" has provided little real comfort to the majority of the population. The last two decades in China have, in fact, witnessed something of a breakdown in the society's value system and moral code. The increasing gap between rich and poor, growing social unrest and perceived injustices, rampant corruption, and an apparently insatiable greed has led millions of Chinese on a search for answers as to how to pursue a happy and balanced life in the whirlpool of a fast-changing world.

It is in this social and political context that the ancient sage has once again been called upon to come to the rescue, led by the media-savvy Yu Dan whose very accessible interpretation of Confucian wisdom has warmed the hearts of millions.

This English edition, titled *Confucius from the Heart*, is a translation of Professor Yu Dan's bestselling Chinese book. Rather than a word-for-word annotation of the original *Analects*, Yu provides us with her own understanding of the ancient wisdom in relation to the trials and tribulations of everyday life. Drawing on her extensive training in the Chinese classics, she regales the reader with quotes from ancient sages, fables and folk tales, lively anecdotes of daily life, and her own personal insights on life and society. The result is a gem of wisdom and sound advice that can benefit anyone in their dealings with a fast-changing world—not just people in China.

天地人之道

心灵之道

处世之道

交友之道

理想之道

人生之道

FOREWORD

Why Confucius?

More than 2,500 years ago, the students of the thinker and philosopher Confucius wrote down every scrap and scattered fragment of his life story and teachings that they could find. These records, based for the most part on classroom notes, were compiled and edited, and afterward they became what we know as *The Analects of Confucius. Analects* simply means a collection of miscellaneous writings.

Just over two thousand years ago, the great Han Dynasty emperor Wu rejected a hundred other philosophical schools in favor of Confucius, effectively making China a Confucian state.

A thousand years ago the first prime minister of the Song Dynasty, Zhao Pu, boasted that he could rule the known world with just half a book of the *Analects*. From this we can see the tremendously important role that Confucius played in the political and social life of ancient times, and the high esteem in which his collected teachings were held by the ancients.

But what practical meaning do they have for our society and our lives today?

When I entrusted the manuscript of my book to the Zhonghua Book Company in China at the end of 2006, I was content but also a little troubled. I started my master's degree in pre–Qin Dynasty literature at the age of twenty-one, and I had grown up immersed in books from the Zhonghua Book Company, but I would never have dreamed that one day this elite publishing house would bring out a book of mine, no more than I would have presumed to hope I would ever stand up and talk about *The Analects of Confucius* on television.

I have always respected this book rather than feared it, and my feelings toward it have always been plain, simple, and warm.

Once, in a small town in north China famous for its hot springs, I saw something called the "Ask Sickness Spring." It is said that anybody who takes a comfortable soak in its water will at once understand the source of their illness: people with arthritis will get a tingling feeling in their joints, those with gastrointestinal problems will experience a hot sensation in their gut, and people with skin complaints will feel a pleasant flush all over their skin, as if a layer of skin were being washed away, like the sloughed-off skin of a cicada.

For me, the wisdom of Confucius is just such a spring of warm, living water.

With my limited knowledge, even if I truly wanted to write an in-depth analysis of Confucius, I would never, ever dare to do such a thing. It would be like sending me off to make a chemical analysis of that hot spring, when I am totally unequipped to do so. The only possible role for me is that of someone who has been immersed in the spring myself, testing it with my own body and blood, like the thousands and thousands of people who over the last two hundred years and more have steeped themselves in that hot spring and experienced its gifts.

The good will see goodness in it, and the wise will see wisdom. Perhaps the value of this classical text is not in rituals and reverence that inspire awe and fear, but in its inclusiveness and fluidity, the wisdom in which so many people have immersed themselves down the ages, so that every individual, though perceiving it differently, and following different paths, can arrive at last at the same final goal. In China we say "The truth has never been far away from ordinary people" and here that is certainly the case.

It seems to me that the sages never used obscure classical quotations to intimidate people, nor did they load their writing with fancy phrases and difficult words to shut them out. Confucius said: "I am thinking of giving up speech." Zigong said hastily: "If you did not speak, what would there be for us, your disciples, to transmit?" Confucius said, calmly and matter-of-factly, "What does Heaven ever say? Yet there are the four seasons going round and there are the hundred things coming into being. What does Heaven ever say?"

The easy truths of this world can enter into people's hearts because they have never been about indoctrination, but rather are an inner call to wake up every heart and soul.

The reason why these simple truths have survived down the millennia is that they have helped generation after generation of Chinese to stay grounded, to understand the nation and the culture that formed them, and not to lose their heads, even when confronted by immense social change and almost overwhelming choice.

Those who benefit from the wisdom of Confucius may experience a moment's heart-stopping enlightenment, in which understanding suddenly floods through them; equally, they may undertake a lifetime of endless study in order to attain understanding.

I must thank the television program *Lecture Room* for encouraging me to approach Confucius from this angle of *xinde*—an understanding that comes from the heart as much as the head. A thousand hearts will get a thousand different things out of his work, ten thousand will get ten thousand different things from it, and mine is no more than the understanding of one heart among many. When we read it in the course of our lives today, and everything suddenly becomes clear to us, Confucius must surely be smiling silently on us from across the centuries.

Zhao Pu's boast is a respectful acknowledgment of Confucius as the source of Chinese traditional culture and thought. I, however, would rather say, "With half a book of the *Analects* I can enrich myself." Everybody should see it as a warm, gentle "Ask Sickness Spring."

Thus what we can learn from Confucius today is not the "Confucian learning" set out by Emperor Wu; it is not the solemn, dignified, ritualized "Confucian religion" that stands alongside Daoism and Buddhism in China; nor is it the Confucianism of the scholars, full of deep argumentation and fettered by textual research.

What we can take away from *The Analects of Confucius* are the simple truths that every person knows in his or her heart, though they may not let them out through their mouths.

In my view, the wisdom of Confucius does not burn your hands, nor is it icy cold. Its temperature is just slightly above body heat, for it is a constant that will remain the same throughout the ages.

Midnight, November 16, 2006

PART ONE

The Way of Heaven and Earth

You should not think that the wisdom of Confucius is lofty and out of reach, or something that people today can only look up to with reverence.

The truths of this world are forever plain and simple, in the same way that the sun rises every day in the east, just as spring is the time for sowing and autumn is the time to harvest.

The truths that Confucius gives us are always the easiest of truths.

They tell us all how we can live the kind of happy life that our spirit needs.

The wisdom of Confucius can help us to obtain spiritual happiness in the modern world, to get used to the daily routine of our lives, and to find the personal bearings that tell us where we are.

We might sometimes think that what we read lacks a rigorous logic. Very many of the sayings concentrate on a single issue, there are few passages of any great length, and almost everything we find is simple and short.

We will see how this absence of words is also a kind of teaching.

Confucius said, "What does Heaven ever say? Yet there are the four seasons going round and there are the hundred things coming into being. What does Heaven ever say?" (*Analects* XVII). Confucius said: See, the heavens are above us, solemn and quiet, never speaking a word, yet the four seasons come round again and again, and all of nature increases and multiplies around us. Do the heavens need to speak as well?

What we will find in Confucius is a way of thinking that is plain, simple, and warm. It is exactly this attitude with which Confucius influenced his students.

Confucius had three thousand students, seventy-two of whom were men of exceptional wisdom and virtue. Each of these men was a seed, and each in his turn spread the seed of this wisdom and this view of life far and wide.

That is why in China we call Confucius a sage. The sages are those people who in their time on this earth are the most practical and capable, and possess the most personal magnetism. They bring us conviction, and a kind of faith. Such men can only be the product of natural growth, emerging from within our lives, not dropping down from heaven.

This sense of natural, balanced growth can be found in China's creation myth, which tells of Pan Gu, who separated heaven and earth. This separation was not a sudden change, as in a Western creation myth, where Pan Gu might be expected to take a big ax and split them apart with a bang, whereupon a golden light might shine out in all directions, and the heavens, earth, and everything in them all appear at once. That is not the Chinese style.

The type of story that Chinese people are used to is like that described in the *San Wu Li Ji,* our very early Chinese history, which includes stories of how the world was made. Here we find that creation was a very lengthy process: calm, relaxed, and full of anticipation:

> *Heaven and earth were jumbled together in a cosmic egg for eighteen thousand years, and Pan Gu lived in the midst of it. The heavens and the earth split apart. The pure Yang essence became the heavens, the heavy Yin essence was the earth. Pan Gu was between them, nine changes in one day, a god in the heavens and a sage on the earth. Every day the heavens rose higher by ten feet, the earth grew thicker by ten feet, and Pan Gu became ten feet taller. When he reached eighteen thousand years of age, the heavens were infinitely high, the earth was infinitely deep, and Pan Gu was infinitely tall.*

Afterward, heaven and earth split apart, not in the way that a solid body splits in two with a crack, but rather as a gradual separation of two essences: the light, pure *yang* essence rose up and became the heavens, and the heavy *yin* essence sank and became the earth.

But that was not the end of the separation of heaven and earth. The process had only just begun.

Notice how Chinese people pay a lot of attention to changes. Look at Pan Gu, who in between the heavens and the earth went through "nine changes in one day": just like a newborn baby, tiny, subtle changes were taking place every day.

There is a stage in the changes that the text calls "a god in the heavens, a sage on earth," when Pan Gu had become a wise and powerful being in both realms.

For the Chinese, this idea of mastery in both realms is an ideal way of being, one to which we should all aspire: a heaven where idealism can spread its wings and fly freely, with no need to compromise with all the rules and obstacles of the real world; and the ability to keep our feet planted firmly on the ground, so that we can make our way in the real world.

People who have only ambition and no realism are dreamers, not idealists; those who have only earth and no sky are plodders, not realists.

Idealism and realism are our heaven and earth.

But Pan Gu's changes are still going on and our story continues.

After the heavens and the earth had separated, every day the heavens became higher by ten feet, the earth gained ten feet in thickness, and Pan Gu "became ten feet taller" every day, along with the heavens.

In this way another eighteen thousand years passed, until at last "the heavens were infinitely high, the earth was infinitely deep, and Pan Gu was infinitely tall."

In other words, humankind is equal to the heavens and the earth: heaven, earth, and people are referred to together as the Three Realms—the three equally great and important things from which the world is made.

Confucius viewed the world in this way: human beings are worthy of respect, and people should respect themselves.

When reading *The Analects of Confucius* we find that Confucius very seldom spoke harshly or sternly to his students; he usually talked things over with them in a relaxed, easy manner, giving them clues and hints so that they could work things out for themselves. We have all seen teachers scold their students, telling them not to do this or that. That is what happens when a teacher is not all he or she should be. A truly excellent teacher will be like Confucius, peacefully exchanging views with their students, together getting to the heart of how to make these Three Realms of heaven, earth, and humanity all prosper and flourish together.

This relaxed, unhurried, assured spirit and modest, respectful attitude is something we should all aspire to. *The Analects of Confucius* is the embodiment of this ideal.

From it we can derive great strength, a strength that flowed from Confucius's inner heart. It is this strength that Mencius, another of China's great philosophers, who came after Confucius and further developed his ideas, described as "the noble spirit."

Only when the essences of heaven, earth, and everything in between combine within a person's heart can they be as powerful as this.

Our ultimate aim is to let the key principles of Confucius enter into our hearts, uniting heaven, earth, and humankind in a perfect whole, and giving us infinite strength.

In China today we often say that for a nation to survive and prosper, heaven must smile on it, the earth must be favorable to it, and its people must be at peace. It is to this harmonious balance that Confucius can lead us today.

What do we mean by heaven and humanity becoming one? We mean humankind and the natural world in perfect harmony.

We are working hard to create a harmonious society, but what is true harmony? It is more than just harmony within a small housing estate, or mere cordial relations between people. It must also include the entire natural world, harmoniously and happily living and growing together on this earth. People should feel reverence for the natural world and a willingness to follow its rhythms.

This is a kind of strength. If we learn how to temper this strength, and to draw on it, then we will be able to attain a breadth of mind like that of Confucius.

Confucius's attitude was extremely placid, yet his inner heart was very serious. This was because he had a deep strength within him, rooted in the strength of his convictions.

His student Zigong once asked him what conditions were necessary for a country to be at peace, with a stable government. Confucius's reply was very simple. There were only three: enough arms, enough food, and the trust of the common people.

First, the internal apparatus of the state must be powerful; it must have enough military power to protect itself.

Second, it must have sufficient supplies, so its people can be well fed and clothed.

Third, the common people must have belief in the nation.

This student was always full of awkward questions. He said that three conditions were too many: Tell me, if you have to do without one of these, which one would you remove first?

Confucius said: "Give up arms." So we'll do without military protection.

Zigong asked again: If you had to get rid of another one, which would you give up?

Confucius in all seriousness told him: "Give up food." We are willing not to eat.

He continued: "Death has always been with us since the beginning of time, but when there is no trust, the common people will have nothing to stand on."

To do without food will certainly lead to death, but from ancient times to this day has anyone ever cheated death? So death is not the worst thing that can happen. The most terrible thing of all is the collapse and breakdown that follow when a country's citizens give up on their nation.

On a material level, a happy life is no more than a series

of goals to be reached; but true peace and stability come from within, from an acceptance of those that govern us, and this comes from faith.

This is Confucius's concept of government. He believed that the power of faith alone was sufficient to hold a nation together.

In the twenty-first century we say that it is no longer enough to use the simplistic standard of GNP (Gross National Product) to assess the quality of the people's life in different countries. You must also look at GNH: Gross National Happiness.

In other words, to evaluate whether a country is truly rich and powerful, you should not just look at the speed and scale of its economic growth, you should look more at the feelings in the heart of each ordinary citizen—Do I feel safe? Am I happy? Do I truly identify with the life I lead?

At the end of the 1980s, China took part in an international survey, which showed that at that time the happiness of our citizens was only around 64 percent.

In 1991 we took part in the survey again. The happiness index had risen, reaching around 73 percent. This came from an improvement in our standard of living, as well as all the reforms that were being carried out around then.

But by the time we took part for a third time, in 1996, the happiness index had fallen to 68 percent.

This is a very puzzling business. It shows that even when a society is thriving materially and culturally, the people who enjoy the fruits of that society may nonetheless experience an extremely complex kind of spiritual bewilderment.

Confucius said: "I am thinking of giving up speech." Zigong said: "If you did not speak, what would there be for us, your disciples, to transmit?" The Master said: "What does Heaven ever say? Yet there are the four seasons going round and there are the hundred things coming into being. What does Heaven ever say?"

—ANALECTS XVII

Let us travel back in time two thousand five hundred years, and compare what the sages and wise men were like in that less prosperous age.

Confucius was very fond of a student called Yan Hui. On one occasion he praised him: "How admirable Hui is! Living in a mean dwelling on a bowlful of rice and a ladleful of water is a hardship most men would find intolerable, but Hui does not allow this to affect his joy. How admirable Hui is!" (*Analects* VI).

Yan Hui's family was very poor. They never had enough to eat or new clothes to wear, and lived in a grim, run-down little alley. For most people, a hard life like this would be simply unendurable, yet Yan Hui could find happiness in what he had.

Perhaps many people would say: "That's just the way life is. We all have to live, rich or poor; what can be done about it?"

What is truly admirable about Yan Hui is not that he could endure such rough living conditions, but rather his attitude to life. When everybody was sighing bitterly and complaining about how hard life is, Yan Hui's optimism never wavered.

We see that only the truly enlightened can avoid becoming tied down by the material things in life and keep a calm, tranquil mind-set from start to finish, indifferent to fame or personal gain.

Of course, nobody wants to live a hard life, but equally, we cannot solve our spiritual problems through a dependence on more and more possessions.

In modern China, our lives are visibly improving in a material sense, yet a great many people are growing more and more dissatisfied. Because we have a highly visible class of people who have suddenly become extremely wealthy, there is always something to make ordinary people feel that their lives contain unfairness.

Everybody hopes to live a happy life, but happiness is only a feeling, which has nothing to do with wealth or poverty, but with the inner heart. Confucius tells his students how to look for happiness in life. This philosophy has been passed down over the ages, and had a profound influence on a great many of our famous scholars and poets.

Actually, what we focus on can work in two ways: one is outward-looking, infinitely broad, expanding our world; another is inward-looking, delving infinitely deep to explore the inner heart.

We always spend too much time looking at the outside world, and too little looking at our hearts and souls.

Confucius can teach us the secret of happiness, which is how to find the peace within us.

A student, Zigong, once asked Confucius: "'Poor without being obsequious, wealthy without being arrogant.' What do you think of this saying?" Imagine somebody who is very poor but doesn't grovel to the rich, or someone who is very rich and powerful but not haughty or arrogant. What do you think of that?

Confucius told him this is pretty good, but it is still not enough. There is another, higher state: "poor yet delighting in the Way, wealthy yet observant of the rites."

The higher state requires that a person not only accept poverty peaceably, and not go crawling and begging for favors, but also possess a calm, clear inner happiness, the kind of happiness that cannot be taken away by a life of poverty. Neither will power and riches make such a person haughty or self-indulgent: they will still be refined and courteous, with a cheerful, contented mind. Such a person can both avoid being led astray by a life of wealth and plenty as well as keep their self-respect and inner happiness. Such a person can truly be called a *junzi*.

The word *junzi,* which appears more often than any other in *The Analects of Confucius,* describes Confucius's ideal person, who any one of us, rich or poor, has the potential to become. To this day, in China, we still use the word as a standard for personal integrity, saying that such and such a person is a real *junzi*. As Confucius's ideas were passed down the generations, they shaped the many great-hearted *junzi* who appear throughout our history and whom we can learn from as we strive to become *junzi* in our own lives.

Tao Yuanming, the great poet of the Eastern Jin Dynasty, was one such figure. For eighty-three days he held a minor official post of magistrate of Pengze, until one very small thing led him to reject his post and return home.

He was told that his superiors were sending someone to inspect his work and that he should "tie your robes with a belt to greet him," just as today you would wear a suit and tie to show respect to visiting leaders.

Our eyes see too much of the world, and too little of the heart and soul.

Tao Yuanming said: "I can't bow low like a servant for the sake of five measures of rice." In other words, he was not prepared to grovel for the sake of an official's tiny salary. And so he went back home, leaving his seal of office behind.

When he got there, he wrote down what he felt.

He said: "Since my heart has become the slave of my body, I feel melancholy and grieved." He felt that just in order to eat a little better and have somewhere slightly better to live, he had no choice but to abase himself, grovel, and curry favor.

He was not willing to live such a life—"I know that I cannot return to my past, but I know my own future and can pursue it"—and so he returned once more to his beloved countryside.

In modern people's eyes, to be content to be poor while holding fast to one's principles tends to imply a certain lack of get-up-and-go. Everybody is working hard to develop their own career in the face of fierce competition, and it seems that how much a person earns, and their professional status (or lack of it), have become the most important signs of success.

But the fiercer the competition, the more we need to adjust our outlook, and our relationships with others. With this in mind, how should we conduct ourselves in modern society? Are there rules to guide us?

Zigong again asked Confucius an extremely important question: "Is there a single word that can be a guide to conduct throughout one's life?" Can you give me one word that I will be able to use until the end of my days, and always derive benefit from it?

Confucius replied to him in a conversational tone of voice: "If such a word exists, it is probably the word *shu,* or 'forbearance.'"

But what do we mean by this? Confucius went on: "Do not impose on others what you yourself do not desire." That is, you mustn't force other people to do the things you don't want to do yourself. If a person can do this throughout their life, that is enough.

And this is what is meant by "With half a book of *The Analects of Confucius* I can govern the Empire." Sometimes learning one word or a couple of words is enough to last us a whole lifetime.

Confucius is a true sage—he won't give you so very much to remember, and sometimes a single word is all you need.

Confucius's disciple Zengzi once said: "The way of the Master consists in doing one's best and in using oneself as a measure to gauge others. That is all." The essence of Confucius's teaching can be distilled into just two words: *faithfulness* and *forbearance*. Put simply, you have to be yourself, but at the same time you must think about others.

By forbearance, Confucius means that you mustn't force people to do things against their will, nor must you do things to hurt others. By extension, he means that if other people do things that hurt you, you must do the best you can to treat them with tolerance.

But this is often easier said than done. Often, when something unfair or unjust happens, we can't help brooding, going over it constantly. And by doing so, we are hurt over and over again.

There is an interesting tale in Buddhism.

Two monks came down from their mountain temple to beg alms. When they reached the bank of a river, they saw a girl, who was upset because she was unable to cross it. The old monk said to the girl: "I'll carry you over on my back." And he gave the girl a piggyback ride across the river.

The young monk was too shocked to do anything more than gape in astonishment. He didn't dare to ask any questions. They walked on for another twenty leagues, and at last he could bear it no longer, so he asked the old monk: "Master, we're monks, we're supposed to be celibate. How could you carry a girl across the river on your back?"

The old monk said coolly: "You saw how I got her across the river and then put her down. How come you have carried this thought with you for twenty leagues and yet you still haven't put it down?"

The moral of this story is exactly what Confucius teaches us: When it's time to put things down, put them down. By being tolerant of others, you are in fact leaving yourself a lot more room.

But what Confucius tells us is not just that we should let ourselves pick things up or let them drop, but that we also should do everything we can to give help to those who need it. This is what we mean by "If you give a rose, the scent will remain on your hands": giving can bring more happiness than receiving.

> *Confucius said: "A benevolent man helps others to take their stand insofar as he himself wishes to take his stand, and gets others there insofar as he himself wishes to get there. The ability to take as analogy what is near at hand can be called the method of benevolence."*
>
> —ANALECTS *VI*

Being tolerant of others is actually leaving yourself a lot more room.

There is a third word, besides *faithfulness* and *forbearance,* at the very center of Confucian theory: *benevolence.*

Confucius's student Fan Chi once respectfully asked his teacher: "What is benevolence?" The teacher answered in two words: "Loving people." Loving other people is benevolence.

Fan Chi asked again: "What is this thing called wisdom?" The teacher said: "Knowing people." The understanding of others is called wisdom.

To love and care for others is benevolence; to understand others is wisdom. It's as simple as that.

So what is the best way to be a person with a benevolent, loving heart?

If you wish to raise yourself up, immediately think of how to help other people raise themselves up, too; if you want to realize your own ambition, think at once of how to help other people to realize their ambitions. This can be done starting with the small things near to you, treating others as you would like to be treated yourself. This is the way to live according to benevolence and justice.

In life, any one of us may experience sudden unemployment, marriage breakdown, betrayal by a friend, or abandonment by someone close to us, and we may regard it as either something serious or something minor; there is no objective standard.

For example, if you get a cut, perhaps an inch long, does this count as a severe injury, or a minor one? A delicate, sensitive young girl might make a fuss about something like this for a whole week; but a big, tough young man might simply not notice, from when the cut was made to when it healed by itself.

So, whether we take on the role of a delicate "young girl" or a strong "young man" is something that is entirely up to us.

If you have an infinitely broad mind, you will always be able to keep things in their proper perspective.

I remember a story from my university English coursebook, about a king who spent every day pondering three ultimate questions: Who is the most important person in this world? What is the most important thing? When is the most important time to do things?

He put these three questions to his court and his ministers, but nobody could give him an answer and so he was very downhearted.

Afterward, one day he went out dressed as a commoner and walked to a remote place, where he took shelter for the night in an old man's house.

In the middle of the night, he woke with a start to hear a racket outside, and he saw that a man covered in blood had rushed into the old man's home.

That man said: "There are men after me, they're going to arrest me!" The old man said: "Then take shelter with me here for a while," and hid him away.

The king was too frightened to sleep, and soon he saw soldiers come running up, hot on the trail. The soldiers asked the old man if he had seen anyone come past. The old man said: "I don't know. There's nobody else here."

To love and care for other people is benevolence; to understand other people is wisdom.

Afterward the soldiers went away. The man they had been chasing said a few words of gratitude and left. The old man shut the door and went back to sleep.

The next day the king said to the old man: "Why weren't you afraid to take in that man? Weren't you afraid of causing terrible trouble? It might have cost you your life! And then you just let him go like that. Why didn't you ask who he was?"

The old man said calmly: "In this world, the most important person is the person in front of you who needs your help, the most important thing is to help them, and the most important time is right now; you can't delay, not even for an instant."

It all suddenly became clear to the king: those three philosophical questions he had been pondering for so long were solved in that instant.

This story can also be used as a footnote to reading Confucius.

What is most significant about people like Confucius or any of the other great thinkers from China and abroad, past and present, is that they drew, from their own practical experiences of life, truths and principles that everybody can use.

These truths are not found in the pages of massive volumes of the classics and ancient records, the kind you need a magnifying glass and an enormous dictionary to read and that will take you a lifetime's laborious study to understand.

The true sages wouldn't put on airs or speak with a stern, forbidding face. They have passed down to us their living, breathing experience of human life, through all the great, sweeping changes the world has gone through, so that we can still feel its warmth. From a thousand years ago, they are smiling down on us, watching us in silence as we continue to reap the benefits of their words.

Confucius offers us simple truths that will help us develop our inner hearts and souls and allow us to make the right choices as we go through life's journey. The first step on this journey is having the right attitude.

PART TWO

The Way of the Heart and Soul

As we move through life, it is hard for us to avoid things that cause regret and disappointment. We may lack the strength to change this, but what we can change is the attitude with which we approach these setbacks.

One of the most important things about Confucius is that he tells us how to face regret and suffering with a tranquil mind.

But can wisdom from two and a half millennia ago truly unravel the knots and tangles in the hearts of people today?

We are on this planet for a whole lifetime, so how can our lives be free from regret? In this life, people will always find something or other that does not go as they would wish.

Confucius had three thousand students, of whom seventy-two were men of unusual wisdom and virtue, and every single one of these students had things that grieved him. So how did they view the regrets of human life?

One day, Confucius's student Sima Niu said sorrowfully: "Everybody else has brothers. Why am I the only one without?"

His classmate Zixia consoled him, saying: "I have heard it said: Life and death are a matter of Destiny; wealth and honor depend on Heaven. The *junzi* is reverent and does nothing amiss, is respectful toward others and observant of the rites, and all within the Four Seas are his brothers. What need is there for the *junzi* to worry about not having any brothers?"

These words can be read on several different levels.

Since life and death, wealth and prestige, and all such things are determined by fate, they are beyond our control. We must learn how to accept them and go along with our fate.

But by improving our outlook it is possible for us to keep a sincere and respectful heart, to reduce the mistakes in our words and actions, and ensure we treat others with courtesy and respect.

If you can make a good job of being yourself, then all over the world people will love and respect you like a brother.

Therefore, if you are a true, cultivated *junzi,* why grieve that you have no brothers?

These words, although they did not come from Confucius's own mouth, represent one of the values he advocates.

You must first be able to face squarely up to the regrets in your life, and to accept them in as short a time as possible. You must not get caught up in the middle of your regret, bewailing fate and asking why over and over again—this can only add to your pain.

Second, you must do as much as possible to make up for this regret, by setting out to do the things you *can* do.

This acknowledgment of the unsatisfactory parts of life, and the ability to make up for these lacks through one's own efforts, is precisely the attitude with which Confucius tells us to approach the regrets in our lives.

If a person cannot accept these regrets, what kind of consequences will this lead to in the future?

A single regret can become magnified out of all proportion. And what is the result? As the Indian poet Tagore said: "If you shed tears when you miss the sun, you also miss the stars."

In an old magazine I once read a story about a British tennis player, Gem Gilbert.

When she was small, Gem witnessed a tragedy. One day she went with her mother on a routine visit to the dentist. She thought that she and her mother would be home in no time. But something went very wrong indeed and the poor little girl watched her mother die in the dentist's chair.

This dark memory never left her and there seemed to be nothing she could do to erase it. But the one thing she could do was avoid ever going to the dentist herself.

Years later she became a wealthy and successful tennis player. One day she had such an agonizing toothache that she could take no more. Her family eventually persuaded her she had to do something. "Just get a dentist to come to the house. We don't have to go to the clinic. Your doctor is here, we will stay with you, what's to be scared of?" And so they called a dentist to her home.

But something unexpected happened: after the dentist had set up his equipment and was preparing for surgery, he turned around to find that Gem Gilbert was dead.

This is the strength of psychological suggestion. A single regret can become so magnified that it hangs over you, affecting your whole life. If your life is haunted by regrets from which you cannot free yourself, these regrets can actually damage you physically as well as emotionally.

Since it is impossible to avoid regrets in our lives, the attitude we adopt toward these regrets is extremely important. A different attitude can result in a completely different quality of life.

For example, in a certain small town there lived a very poor girl. She had lost her father, and she and her mother depended on each other for everything, scraping a meager living from handicrafts. She suffered from terrible feelings of inferiority, because she had never had any pretty clothes or trinkets to wear.

On the Christmas when she was eighteen, her mother did something she had never done before and gave her a purse of money, telling her to buy herself a present.

Such a treat was far beyond the girl's wildest dreams, but she still lacked the courage to stroll naturally along. As she walked toward the shops, the purse clutched in her hand, she went out of her way to avoid the crowds, and stuck close to the wall.

On the way there she saw that all the people had better lives than her, and lamented to herself: I can't hold my head up here, I'm the shabbiest girl in this town. When she saw the young man she secretly admired more than any other, she wondered mournfully who his partner would be at the big dance to be held that night.

And so, creeping along and avoiding other people all the way, she reached the shop. As soon as she was inside, something caught her eye: a display of extremely pretty hair decorations.

While she was standing there in a daze, the shop assistant said to her: "What lovely golden hair you have! Try a pale green flower to go with it. You'll look just beautiful." She saw the price tag. It would have cost almost all her money, so she said: "I can't afford it; don't bother." But by then the shop assistant had already fastened that ornament to her hair.

The shop assistant brought a mirror and held it up to the girl. When she saw herself in the mirror, she was amazed. She had never seen herself like this, her face glowing with health and beauty; she felt as if the flower had transformed her into an angel! Without a moment's hesitation, she got out her money and bought it. Giddy with excitement in a way she had never felt before, she took her change, turned around, and rushed outside, colliding with an old man who had just come in through the door. She thought that she heard him call out to her, but she was past worrying about all that, and hurtled out, her feet barely touching the ground.

Before she realized what she was doing, she had run all the way to the main street of the town. She saw that everyone was casting surprised glances in her direction, and she heard them discussing her, saying: "I never knew there was such a pretty girl in this town. Whose daughter is she?" She met the boy she secretly liked again, and to her surprise he called out to her to stop, saying: "Would you do me the honor of being my partner at the Christmas dance?"

The girl was wild with joy! She thought, I'll be extravagant for once—I'll go back and get myself a little something with the change. And with that, she flew elatedly back to the shop.

As soon as she came through the door, that old man said to her with a smile: "I knew you'd be back! Just now when you bumped into me, your flower fell off. I've been waiting all this time for you to come back for it."

This is where the story ends. The pretty hair clip had not really made up for all the sadness in the girl's life; her new self-confidence was what made all the difference.

And where does self-confidence come from? It comes from a practical and steady sense of inner calm, an easy unhurried bearing that is the mark of the true *junzi*.

Confucius's student Sima Niu once asked him: "What sort of person can be called a *junzi*?"

Confucius replied: "The *junzi* is free from worries and fears."

Sima Niu asked again: "So if someone has no worries or fears, he can be called a *junzi*?"

He perhaps thought that this standard was too low.

Confucius said: "If he looks within himself, and sees nothing to make him ashamed or uneasy, of course there is nothing for him to worry about or to be afraid of."

Today, we could use a common folk saying to interpret Confucius's meaning: "If your conscience is clear, you won't be frightened by a midnight knock on your door."

Arguably, reflecting on one's own conduct, and not being able to find anything to regret or be ashamed of, could seem like quite a low standard. In some ways it is. Any one of us could do it. Equally, though, it could be rightly seen as the highest possible standard. Think about it: living so that every single thing we have ever done can stand up to scrutiny is a great challenge. That is why Confucius made it the standard for being a *junzi*.

How then do we achieve this sort of strong inner heart, which can help us live free from worry, indecision, and fear?

If you want to achieve a strong inner heart, you must be indifferent to gains and losses, especially of the material kind. Confucius sometimes referred to people who care too much about gains and losses as "the small men" and denounced them as "petty," in other words, small-minded and second-rate people.

Confucius once said: "Can you let this kind of petty individual plan great matters of state?" No. When someone like this has failed to gain advantage, they complain about not being able to gain it; when they have got what they want, they are afraid of losing it. Since they are afraid of losing, they will stop at nothing to protect what they have and to try to gain more.

A person who is obsessed with personal gains and losses can never have an open heart, or a calm, unperturbed mind, nor can they have true courage.

What is true courage? How does it differ from reckless foolhardiness? And what does Confucius have to say on the subject of courage?

Confucius had a disciple called Zilu, a very impulsive man who cared a lot about matters of courage.

Confucius once said ironically: "If one day my Great Way becomes unworkable, I will end up alone on a boat, floating on the seas and rivers. If anyone is still following me by then, it will probably be Zilu."

Zilu was very pleased with himself when he heard this. But his teacher added: "I say this because apart from courage, Zilu has nothing else." Love of courage was Zilu's defining quality, but his bravery was of the shallow, thoughtless kind.

The Master said: "In the eating of coarse rice and drinking of water, the using of one's elbow for a pillow, joy is to be found. Wealth and rank attained through immoral means have as much to do with me as passing clouds."

—ANALECTS VII

But another day, Zilu asked his teacher: "Does the *junzi* consider courage a supreme quality?"

Confucius said to him: "For the *junzi* it is morality that is supreme. Possessed of courage but devoid of morality, a *junzi* will make trouble while a small man will be a brigand."

What this means is that it is not wrong for a *junzi* to value courage, but it must be a controlled, restrained kind of courage; it has a precondition, which is "morality." Only bravery that puts morality first is true courage. Otherwise, a *junzi* could use their bravery to stir up trouble, and a petty person might even sink to becoming a robber.

If you think about it, robbers and bandits break into houses, commit robbery and even murder, but can you say that they are not brave? However, this bravery unrestrained by morality is the most harmful thing in the world.

So what is "morality" and how do we know what is right and what is wrong?

It is clear that it is a kind of inner restraint. Confucius said: "It is rare for a man to miss the mark through holding on to essentials!" (*Analects* IV). In other words, if a person has this inner restraint, then they will make many fewer mistakes throughout their life.

If a person can truly manage to "examine themselves on three counts" every day (*Analects* I). If you can truly reach the state in which "when you meet someone better than yourself, you turn your thoughts to becoming his equal. When you meet someone not as good as you are, look within and examine your own self" (*Analects* IV). Then you will have achieved restraint. To be able to reflect on one's own failings and work bravely to put them right, this is the true courage promoted by Confucius and his followers.

Many years later, the writer and statesman Su Shi described this bravery in "On Staying Behind." He called it "great courage" and said:

> *What the ancients called a man of outstanding courage and talent must have self-restraint that surpasses that of ordinary men. There are things that humans cannot endure. When the ordinary man has been shamed, he draws his sword and rushes up to fight; this is not sufficient to be called bravery. There are those of great courage in the world, who when suddenly attacked are not afraid, when criticized without a reason do not become angry. This is because the ambitions of such men are great, and they cherish high and lofty aspirations.*

As Su Shi saw it, the truly courageous had a "self-restraint that surpasses that of ordinary men." They could endure bitter public humiliation, just as the famous general Han Xin had faced public humiliation when he was forced to crawl between a man's legs in a public place rather than waste two lives in a duel to the death. This did not stop him from achieving remarkable successes in battle, winning a series of decisive victories. A man like him would never have reacted on a moment's brave impulse just for the sake of snatching a brief moment of satisfaction. This is because he possessed self-belief that was controlled by reason, and a settled, composed mind; this in turn is because he had a broad mind and high and lofty aspirations.

Su Shi described such a man as someone who "when something unexpected happens they are not afraid." This state of mind is very hard to achieve. We can try to be cultivated and moral people and not cause offense to others, but when others offend us for no reason at all, how can we stop ourselves becoming angry?

For example, if on Monday a man is victim of a sudden, severe, and motiveless beating, on Tuesday he will describe it to all his friends, over and over again; by Wednesday he has sunk into a state of gloom and refuses to see anybody or go anywhere: by Thursday he starts to quarrel with his family over trifles . . .

What does this mean? It means that every time you retell the story, you are beaten again. It means that even after the thing is past, you are still affected by it every day.

When misfortune approaches, the best way to deal with it is to let it pass as quickly as possible. Only in this way can you free more time to do the things that matter more; only then will you live more effectively, and be in better shape emotionally.

There are many things in our lives that are not as we would wish. Sometimes they are neither rational nor fair. We may lack the strength to change them, but we can change our own feelings and attitude. Looking at things in this way, we can say that people see whatever is in their heart. The following story of Su Shi and Foyin shows this.

As we have seen, Su Shi was a man of great achievements. Foyin was a high Buddhist monk, and the two of them often meditated together. Foyin was an honest, simple character, and Su Shi was always baiting him. Su Shi would often feel very pleased with himself over these small victories, and when he got home, he liked to talk about them to his sister Su Xiaomei.

One day the two men were sitting meditating together.

Su Shi asked: "Look, what do I look like?"

Foyin said: "I think you look like a statue of the Buddha."

When Su Shi heard this, he laughed out loud, and said to Foyin: "Do you know what I think you look like sitting there? Just like a pile of cow dung."

Foyin was once again left at a loss for words.

When Su Shi went home he boasted about this to Su Xiaomei.

Su Xiaomei laughed coldly and said to her brother: "How can you meditate with such low understanding? Do you know what people who meditate care about the most? It's all about seeing the heart and the essence: whatever there is in your heart will be there in your eyes. Foyin said you were like a Buddha; that shows that there is a Buddha in his heart. You said that Foyin was like a cowpie, so imagine what there must be in your heart!"

This can be applied to every one of us. Think about it: we all live on the same planet, but some people live warm, happy lives, and others moan and groan all day long. Are their lives really so different?

Actually, it is like half a bottle of wine. A pessimist would say: "What a shame! Such a good bottle of wine and there's only half left!" But an optimist would say: "How lovely! Such a good bottle of wine and there's still half left!" The only difference is in their attitudes.

In today's fiercely competitive society, it is more important now than at any other time in history to maintain a positive state of mind.

We should always remember that, as Confucius said, "The *junzi* is at ease without being arrogant; the petty is arrogant without being at ease." Because a *junzi*'s mind is calm, steady, and brave, their serenity and well-being flow naturally from within; whereas what you see in a petty individual is a façade of haughtiness and self-importance; because their mind is restless and ill at ease.

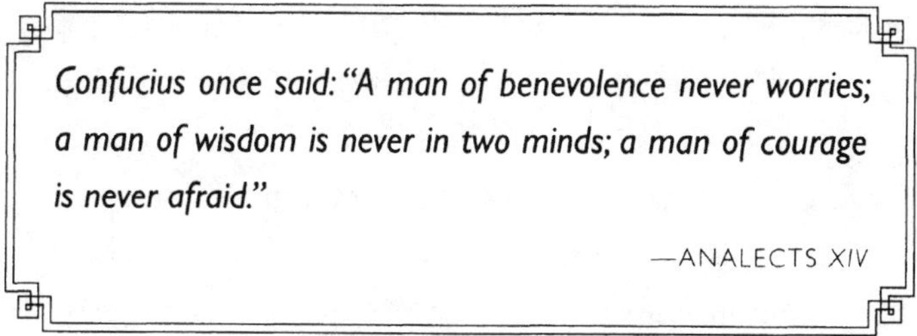

Confucius once said: "A man of benevolence never worries; a man of wisdom is never in two minds; a man of courage is never afraid."

—ANALECTS *XIV*

But Confucius was also very modest. He said that these three things—never worrying, never being in two minds, and never being afraid—were things he had never achieved for himself.

What do we mean by "A man of benevolence never worries"?

That is to say, somebody who has a great heart, full of benevolence and virtue, with an exceptionally kind, tolerant, and generous spirit, will be able to overlook very many small details, and not make a fuss about trifles. Thus he can avoid getting caught up in petty gains and losses. Only this kind of person can truly achieve inner peace and freedom from doubts and fears.

What is meant by "a man of wisdom is never in two minds"?

Just fifty years ago, most Chinese might spend their entire life in just one work unit, divorce was almost unheard of, and they might well live in the same courtyard from childhood to old age. What troubled people was how predictable life was and what little choice there was.

However, today we are troubled not by a lack of choice, but by too many choices. This bafflement and confusion is due to our vibrant, booming society.

We have no control over the external world; all we can do is improve our ability to make choices. When we have understood how to make those choices, how to accept or reject things, these worries and irritations will also cease to exist. This is what Confucius meant by "a man of wisdom is never in two minds."

But what is meant by "a man of courage is never afraid"?

Putting it plainly, we might say: "When two strong men come to blows, the bravest always comes out on top." In other words, when you have sufficient courage and openness, you will be strong enough to move boldly forward, and then you will no longer be afraid.

When a true *junzi* achieves inner benevolence, wisdom, and courage, then their worries, indecision, and fear will all decrease as a result.

I once read a story in a book by the Japanese author Daisetsu Suzuki about a famous tea maker in the Edo period who worked for a powerful and distinguished master. As we all know, Japan promotes the tea ceremony as a part of Zen, in which the tea ceremony and meditation are two parts of one whole.

One day the master decided to go to the capital on business. He could not bear to leave his tea maker behind, so he said to him: "Come with me, so I can drink your tea every day."

But Japan at that time was very dangerous. Bandits and masterless samurai—*ronin*—roamed the countryside, terrorizing the inhabitants.

The tea maker was afraid. He said to his master: "I have no skill with weapons. If I do run into trouble on the road, what will I do?"

His master said: "Carry a sword and dress as a samurai."

The tea maker had no choice. He changed into a samurai's clothes and went with his master to the capital.

One day, the master had gone out to see to his business, so the tea maker went for a walk on his own. At that moment a *ronin* came up to him, and challenged him, saying: "You're a warrior too, I see—let's try your skill against mine."

The tea maker said: "I don't know anything about fighting. I'm just a tea maker."

The *ronin* said: "You are not a samurai, but you're dressed as one. If you have any shame or self-respect at all, you should die by my blade!"

The tea maker racked his brains, but there was clearly no getting out of it, so he said: "Spare me for a few hours so I can complete the tasks my master has given me. This afternoon we'll meet again by the pond."

The *ronin* thought it over and agreed, adding: "Be there, or else."

The tea maker hurried straight to the most famous martial arts school in the capital. He went straight to the chief samurai and said to him: "I beg you, teach me the most honorable way for a samurai to die!"

The chief samurai was extremely surprised. He said: "People come here to seek a living. You're the first one to come seeking death. Why are you doing this?"

The tea maker described his meeting with the *ronin,* and then said: "Making tea is all I know, but today I must engage in mortal combat with that man. I beg you to teach me how. All I want is to die with a little honor."

The chief samurai said: "Very well, you brew me some tea, and then I will tell you what to do."

The tea maker was deeply distressed and said: "This may be the last tea I prepare in this world."

He did it with great concentration, calmly watching the mountain spring water come to the boil on the little stove, then putting in the tea leaves, washing the tea, filtering it, and pouring it out, a little at a time. Then he took a cup in both hands and presented it to the chief samurai.

The chief samurai had been watching the entire process. He tasted a mouthful and said: "This is the best tea I have drunk in my entire life. I can tell you right now that there is no need for you to die."

The tea maker said: "What will you teach me?"

The chief samurai said: "There's no need for me to teach you anything. When you face that *ronin,* all you have to do is remember the state of mind you were in when you made the tea. You don't need anything else."

After the tea maker had heard this he went to keep his appointment. The *ronin* was already waiting for him, and as soon as the tea maker arrived, the *ronin* drew his sword, saying: "Now you're here. Let the duel begin!"

The tea maker had been pondering the words of the great samurai all the way, so he faced this *ronin* in exactly the same state of mind as when he was brewing tea.

He fixed his gaze on his opponent, then unhurriedly removed his hat and placed it squarely beside him. Then he opened his loose outer robe, folded it slowly, and tucked it neatly under the hat; then he produced strips of cloth, and bound the sleeves of his inner garment firmly to his wrists; then he did the same to the cuffs of his trousers. He robed himself for battle from head to foot, remaining calm and unruffled throughout.

The *ronin* was getting anxious. The more he watched the more disconcerted he became, because he could not guess how great his opponent's skill with weapons really was. The look in the other man's eyes and his smile were making him increasingly unsure of himself.

When the tea maker had finished dressing himself, his final action was to draw his sword hissing from its scabbard, and brandish it in midair . . . and there he stopped, because he did not know what to do next.

At that moment the *ronin* threw himself to his knees, crying: "Spare my life, I beg you! I have never seen so skilled a fighter in all my life!"

Was the tea maker's victory really thanks to his fighting skills? No, it was the bravery in his heart, and his relaxed, composed self-confidence. The attitude with which he approached his task.

Technique and skill are not what matter most. To fully comprehend those things that go beyond mere skill, we need to use our hearts and souls.

We can see that the standards of behavior that Confucius has set us are not just an overharsh critique of the world around us; they are about putting our limited time and energy to good use, and turning our criticism inward toward our own hearts and minds.

We should all be a little stricter with ourselves, and a bit more honest and tolerant toward other people. These days we always say that a decent person should be honest and straightforward, but not in the sense of being naïve and too easily manipulated. Instead what matters is the tolerance to forgive others' faults, treat them with compassion, and see things from others' points of view.

For this reason, only true *junzi* can manage "not to blame Heaven, nor to blame Man," neither complaining that fate hasn't given them the lucky break they need, nor bewailing that there is nobody in the world who understands them.

If a person's inner heart is free from worries, indecision, and fear, they will naturally have fewer complaints about the world around them, and their ability to hold on to happiness will also increase.

Increasing our ability to hold on to happiness is the greatest thing we can learn.

A strong heart and soul can make up both for your innate, unavoidable regrets and for the avoidable mistakes you make in life; at the same time it can give you fixity of purpose, raise your spirits, and let you live the fullest, most effective life possible. Every day you will experience a new rebirth, and you will show others the way to experience all these beautiful things.

If you are clearheaded and generous minded, candid and brave, then you may find that you reap many unexpected benefits, and everybody will be willing to tell you all sorts of wonderful things. However, if you are the opposite of this, even a teacher such as Confucius, who taught worthy and unworthy alike, would not waste his breath talking to you.

As Confucius said, if you come across someone who could benefit from what you could tell them but you do not try to talk to them, you are "letting a man go to waste." You have missed your chance with that person, which is not good. Conversely, if this person refuses to listen, your words are going to waste, and this is not good, either.

If you want to be the kind of person whom people are able to talk to, the key is to keep a clear and open mind. In our busy modern world, where society is ever more complex, it is vital that we adopt the broad-minded positive outlook of a *junzi*. Confucius shows us how.

PART THREE

The Way of the World

In the modern world, with e-mail and messaging, we can be constantly in touch with people thousands of miles away, yet we make no effort to get to know our neighbors.

More than ever before, the way we deal with other people is crucial.

In this confused and complicated social environment, how should we treat others?

When someone treats us unfairly, how should we react? What are the principles we should adopt when dealing with the people closest to us?

Confucius gives us many rules on how to conduct ourselves in society and so be a decent person. These rules may at first appear fixed, even rigid, but in fact they contain a surprising flexibility.

Put simply, he gives us the principles that should govern our actions and the degree to which we should follow those principles.

We often ask ourselves what we should do and what we shouldn't; what is good and what is bad.

Actually, when it comes to asking these questions, it very often happens that things cannot be divided according to simple ideas of right and wrong, good and bad, yes and no. When we do something, and the extent to which we do it, will also have a direct influence on how we should act. Confucius particularly stressed how far we should go in doing anything. Acting to excess or not doing enough are both to be avoided, as far as possible.

So, although Confucius advocated benevolence and charity, he did not believe that we should pardon the faults of everybody we meet with indiscriminate benevolence.

Somebody asked him: "What do you think of the saying 'Repay an injury with a good turn'?"

Confucius replied: "You repay an injury with straightness but you repay a good turn with a good turn." This may not be quite what we would have expected to hear, but an awareness of the limits of what is acceptable in others is one key hallmark of the true *junzi*.

What Confucius is advocating here is respect for human dignity.

Of course, he did not suggest repaying one grievance with another grievance. If we constantly confront wrongs done to us with ill will and spite, then we will be caught up in a vicious circle that can never cease. We will sacrifice not only our own happiness, but our grandchildren's, too.

Repaying a grievance with virtue is not practicable, either. If you are too free with your goodness and mercy, treating those who have done you wrong with unnecessary kindheartedness, this, too, is a waste.

But there is a third attitude, which is to face all of this calmly, with fair-mindedness, justice, openness, and uprightness, that is to say, to approach it with a high moral character. By extension, Confucius stressed that we must keep our feelings and our talents for the places where they are needed.

These days everyone is trying to avoid wasting resources, yet we have overlooked the desolation of spirit and waste of energy that occurs within our own bodies every day.

Today's material prosperity and the increasing speed of the rhythms of life require us to make very swift judgments. We have to choose the best way to live, a way that is truly our own.

In our lives, we often see the following perplexing situations:

A father and mother who are good to their child, yet this only drives the child away.

Friends who are as close as close can be, but always seem to end up hurting each other.

A person who schemes with all their might for a closer relationship with superiors and colleagues, yet who frequently achieves the very opposite.

How can this be?

Confucius believed that neither excessive aloofness nor excessive intimacy was ideal. For him "going too far is as bad as not going far enough." Extreme intimacy is not the ideal situation for two people who want to get along.

So how do we achieve "good" relationships?

Confucius's student Ziyou said: "To be importunate with one's lord will mean humiliation. To be importunate with one's friends will mean estrangement." In other words, if you are always hanging around your superiors whether you have any business with them or not, although you are making a show of closeness you will soon bring humiliation upon yourself. Equally, if you are always sticking close to your friend's side, although it appears that you are inseparable, estrangement will not be far away.

There is a fable that illustrates this. There once was a group of porcupines, all covered in sharp spines, huddling together to keep warm over the winter. They could never work out how far apart they should be. Just a little bit too far away and they couldn't keep each other warm, so they crowded closer; but as soon as they squeezed closer together, the sharp spines would prick them, so they started to move farther apart, but once they did, they felt the cold. It took a good deal of trial and error for the porcupines to finally find the right degree of separation, so that they could retain the warmth of the group without hurting each other.

In China today, especially in the big cities, the old multifamily courtyards have all been pulled down and blocks of flats built in their place. Gone are the days when one family would make dumplings and give some to all the neighbors, and we no longer see all the inhabitants of a courtyard celebrate New Year together, one table for the adults, another for the children. Often neighbors who have lived for three or four years on the same staircase don't really know each other.

Because our relationships with the people who live around us have become colder, it is harder to for us to communicate with one another.

This then increases the burden on the few friends we do rely on.

You might think: My best friend should treat me a bit better; then I will go out of my way to be a bit nicer to him. You might think: If you're having family problems, an argument with your partner, for example, why don't you tell me? I can step in and mediate for you!

A lot of us think in this way. But we should listen to Ziyou; excessive closeness is bound to harm other people.

So how should we get on with our friends?

Zigong once asked his teacher this question and Confucius told him: "Advise them to the best of your ability and guide them properly, but stop when there is no hope of success. Do not ask to be snubbed." When you see a friend doing something wrong, you should do your best to warn them off, and guide them with goodwill, but if they really don't listen, let it go. Don't say any more; otherwise you're just making a rod for your own back.

So with good friends you also need boundaries. More is not always better.

Confucius warns us that, whether with friends or leaders, we must keep a certain distance, and know where the boundaries lie between intimacy and estrangement.

So, with our family, who are dearer to us than anyone else, should we be as close as close can be?

Or should we also maintain a certain distance between parents and children, husband and wife, or between lovers?

Psychologists have a term for the kind of behavior that we often see in modern people's interactions—"nonloving behavior." It describes, very accurately, what happens when, in the name of love, people behave in a grasping, coercive way toward those dearest to them. It often happens between husband and wife, between lovers, between mother and son, or father and daughter—in other words, between the people who are closest to one another.

A husband or wife might say to the other: "Just look what I have given up for love of you. I did this or that just for the sake of this family, so now you must treat me a certain way."

Lots of mothers say to their children: "Look—after I had you, I fell behind at work, I lost my looks, I sacrificed everything for you, so why can't you do a bit better at school?"

All of this is nonloving behavior: a sort of coercion in the name of love, to make other people behave the way we want them to.

I once read a book on parenting by a British psychologist who had some very wise things to say:

Love is almost always about bringing people closer together. But there is one kind of love, and one only, whose aim is separation: the love of parents for their children. Truly successful parental love means letting the child become independent and separate from your lives as early as possible; the earlier this separation, the more successful you have been as parents.

Seen like this, independence and a respectful distance are essential to an individual's personal dignity, and this respect should be maintained, even between the people we are closest to.

Whether between fathers and sons, mothers and daughters, or

long-married husbands and wives, once that respectful distance is breached, once you have overstepped the mark, and reached the stage that Confucius calls "importunate," so that you are no longer properly independent of each other, there will be problems. Hidden damage, estrangement, or even a total breakdown in relations will not be far away.

Confucius shows us that we must respect every person equally and rationally, maintain a tactful distance, and give each other breathing space.

This is very much like the Zen Buddhist state called "the flower not fully open, the moon not fully round."

This is the best state that can exist between people. As soon as a flower is fully open, it begins to fade; as soon as the moon is completely full, it starts to wane. But when the flower is not fully open, nor the moon quite full, you will still feel anticipation and have something to long for.

It is always like this, with both friends and family. By giving them room you will find new horizons opening up in front of your eyes.

Whether toward friends or family, we should all know where our limits are. Moderation is best.

So in our work life, is it really true that the more enthusiastic we are the better?

Is it the case that the more work we do, the better, whether it is part of our duty or not?

When dealing with work, are there also limits that we need to understand?

The Master said: "Have the firm faith to devote yourself to learning, and abide to the death in the good way. Enter not a state that is in peril; stay not in a state that is in danger. Show yourself when the Way prevails in the Empire, but hide yourself when it does not. It is a shameful matter to be poor and humble when the Way prevails in the state. Equally, it is a shameful matter to be rich and noble when the Way falls into disuse in the state."

—ANALECTS *VIII*

Many Chinese university students have gained work experience in a foreign enterprise. As soon as you go in, the head of human resources will give you a written *job description,* which describes your position, and the work you will be doing. Everyone has one, from clerks and typists all the way up to the senior management.

In China, we generally fix the type of work we do, but not how much. We are always saying that young people must work hard and well, and one person doing the work of three is the best of all; we believe this will help lighten the load for everyone. This is at odds with the spirit of modern enterprise management. The person responsible for a task should be the one to take care of it; in this way, everybody comes together as part of a coherent strategy.

Confucius said: "Do not concern yourself with matters of government unless they are the responsibility of your office." In other words, whatever position you are in, you must do your duty, you must not exceed your authority and meddle in other people's affairs, stepping beyond your duties to do things you don't have to do. This professional attitude to work is one that our modern society would do well to pay attention to.

However, there is an implied condition here, which is "When they *are* the responsibility of your office, you *must* concern yourself with matters of government." So then, when they are your responsibility, how should you concern yourself with matters of government? How do we know what we should do?

Confucius said: "In his dealings with the world the *junzi* is not invariably for or against anything. He is on the side of what is moral."

What Confucius meant was that the *junzi* doesn't try to force things, doesn't oppose things without a reason, is neither too demanding nor too detached, neither too close nor too distant, but acts morally and justly. Morality and justice should be the principles and standards by which we all conduct ourselves.

Once we know what should guide us in how we act, we should concern ourselves with our actions themselves.

Between "words" and "actions," Confucius set greater store by "actions." He was extremely wary of people who brag and show off.

He said: "It is rare, indeed, for a man with cunning words and an ingratiating face to be benevolent." You cannot find someone of real virtue among the kind of people who are all fine words and ingratiating manner.

So what did Confucius advocate? Very simply—say less, do more. You should be enthusiastic in your actions, but he advises "cautious speech." You must not say you can do something when you can't. As the Chinese folk saying goes, "Troubles come from the mouth," and while this may be putting it a bit strongly, the least you can expect from boasts is "too many words and you lose the meaning."

Confucius's student Zizhang wanted to study in order to become an official.

Zizhang wanted a position of responsibility in society, and he asked his teacher what he should do.

> *Confucius told him: "Use your ears widely but leave out what is doubtful; repeat the rest with caution and you will make few mistakes. Use your eyes widely and leave out what is hazardous; put the rest into practice with caution and you will have few regrets. When in your speech you make few mistakes and in your action you have few regrets, an official career will follow as a matter of course."*
>
> —ANALECTS *II*

"Use your ears widely but leave out what is doubtful" means that you must first use your ears and listen to what people are telling you, but the parts you aren't sure about you should leave to one side. We call learning from what happens to us direct experience, while learning from other people's experiences and the paths they have taken, including their frustrations and misfortunes, is called indirect experience.

"Repeat the rest with caution" means that you should be careful when you discuss what you have heard, even the parts that you think you are sure about. "And you will have few regrets" means just that.

"Use your eyes widely and leave out what is hazardous" means look around you, but again leave things you aren't sure about to one side. Confusion is mostly the result of a limited field of vision: How can a frog at the bottom of a well understand the vastness of the ocean or the sky?

Once you have become rich in experience, you still have to be cautious in your actions. This kind of caution is described as behaving "as if approaching a deep abyss, as if walking on thin ice" (*Analects* VIII).

Think more, listen more, see more, be cautious in your words and in your actions—the advantage of doing things in this way is that you will have fewer regrets.

Nobody in the world sells a cure for regrets. As soon as a person knows they have done something wrong, the thing has become a fait accompli, and there is no way to retrieve it. If a person avoids placing blame and complaining when speaking, and in actions avoids many of the experiences that lead to regrets, they will be sure to succeed in what they set out to do.

There is a story I read on the Internet.

Once there was a bad-tempered little boy who was dreadfully stubborn, flying constantly into rages, smashing and hitting things. One day his father took the child by the hand and led him to the fence at the back of their garden, saying: "Son, from now on, every time you lose your temper at home, bang a nail into the fence. Then after a while you can see how many times you've lost your temper, all right?" The child thought, What's to be afraid of? I'll give it a try. After that, every time he threw a tantrum, he banged a nail into the fence, and when he came a day later to look, he felt a bit embarrassed: "Oh! All those nails! Heaps of them!"

His father said: "Do you see? You have to control yourself. If you manage not to lose your temper for a whole day, you can pull out one of the nails from the fence." The boy thought, If I lose my temper once then I have to hammer in a nail, but I have to go for a whole day without losing my temper before I can pull one out—that's really difficult! And yet, to get rid of the nails, he had to keep himself constantly under control.

At the start, the boy found it terribly difficult, but by the time he had pulled all the nails out of the fence, he suddenly realized that he had learned how to control himself. He went off happily to his father, saying: "Daddy, quick, come and look, there are no more nails in the fence, and I don't lose my temper anymore."

The father went with the boy to stand next to the fence, and said in a voice full of significance: "Look, son, the nails in the fence have all been pulled out, but the holes will stay there forever. Every time you lose your temper with your family, it drives a hole into their hearts. When the nail has been pulled out, you can apologize, but you can never make the hole disappear."

This story is a perfect explanation of what Confucius meant by "in your speech you make few mistakes and in your action you have few regrets."

Before we do a thing, we should pause for a moment to consider the consequences, just as once the nail is hammered in, even if it is pulled out later, the fence can never go back to the way it was before. When we do things, we must take the long view and be doubly cautious. In this way we can avoid hurting other people, and will have fewer regrets in the days to come.

When speaking, we must think carefully; in our actions, we must consider the consequences. This is the most important thing to remember in all our interactions.

If you want to be able to cope with all the different kinds of interpersonal relationships in our diverse and complex modern society, it is more important than ever to understand courtesy.

So how did Confucius understand courtesy?

Confucius set a great deal of store by ceremony in daily life. He respected courtesy, and observed the correct ceremonies, but never just for show; rather, it was as a kind of self-cultivation. When men who held official posts, people dressed in mourning, and blind people went past, he would always stand up, even if the person was younger than him, and so below him in the social hierarchy. If he had to pass in front of these people, he would walk quickly, taking small steps, to show his respect.

This is courtesy.

Confucius behaved like this in other situations as well.

It is said of Confucius: "When drinking at a village gathering, he left as soon as those carrying walking sticks had left." "When the villagers were exorcising evil spirits, he stood in his court robes on the eastern steps [the place for a host to stand]." When the wine-drinking ceremonies held by the villagers finished, Confucius always waited until the old people with walking sticks had gone through the door before leaving himself; he would never barge in front of them.

These are the very smallest of ceremonies. We might even wonder why the writers of the ancient books and records bothered to record a great sage doing such trivial things. Didn't everyone know to do this sort of thing? Isn't this just glorifying the sage?

Actually, the so-called sage's language and actions really were just that simple, so simple that it even makes people today a little bit suspicious. These stories are just like something that might happen in your neighborhood, or in your home.

But how warm they are! It makes us feel that sages are not so far removed from us. Once again, Confucius shows us the truths he uncovered, and the events he experienced, for us to share.

We can therefore see that actions that may outwardly appear insignificant are truly important when they come from the heart and soul.

Confucius's student Zilu once asked his teacher how he could become a *junzi*. Confucius told Zilu: "He cultivates himself and thereby achieves reverence." Cultivate yourself, and maintain a serious, respectful attitude. Zilu's reaction to this: "Just by doing this, you can become a *junzi*? Surely it can't be that simple?"

Confucius added a little more: "He cultivates himself and thereby brings peace to his fellow men." First make yourself a better person; then you can think of ways to make other people happy.

Zilu was plainly not satisfied with this, and pressed him further: "Is that all?"

Confucius continued: "He cultivates himself and thereby brings security to the people. Even Yao and Shun would have found the task of bringing peace and security to the people taxing." Even *junzi* and sages such as Yao and Shun, the wise emperors of legend, would have found such a task hard going. If you can manage all this, you will certainly be good enough to be a *junzi*!

The Analects of Confucius is full of these simple little stories that might have happened to any one of us—we rarely see any long sections of high-flown moralizing. We are not left feeling that the truths Confucius offers us are beyond our reach. Instead they feel very warm, and within our grasp.

What Confucius tells us to focus on first is not how to bring stability to the world, but how to be the best possible version of ourselves. To "cultivate one's moral character" is the first step toward taking responsibility for the nation, and for society. Confucius and his disciples struggled hard to be "the best version" of themselves, but their aim in this was to better carry out their responsibilities to the society in which they lived.

Confucius said: "Men of antiquity studied to improve themselves; men of today study to impress others" (*Analects* XIV). The ancients studied in order to make themselves better people, but today we study in order to show off, and ingratiate ourselves with others.

Someone who has genuine respect for learning studies in order to improve his or her mind. Learning from books, learning from society, learning as we grow from childhood to old age, from all of this you will learn the ability to hold on to happiness.

First make yourself into a loyal, educated, and knowledgeable citizen, then, armed with all this, go to find your place in society and your role in life. The aim of studying is to complete the process of finding your place and improving yourself.

And what is "studying to impress others"?

It is the acquisition of knowledge as a mere tool, a skill that will help you get a job, or some other purely personal benefit.

Confucius never said that you have to be like any one person in order to be a *junzi*. As he saw it, to be a *junzi* is to be the best possible version of yourself, based on where you are right now, beginning with the things around you, and starting today, so that your mind can achieve a state of perfect balance. For it is only when you are possessed of a truly calm, steady, down-to-earth mind and heart that you can avoid being swayed by the rises and falls, gains and losses of life.

This reminds me of a little story:

Three tailors each opened a shop on the same street. Each of them wanted to attract the most customers.

The first tailor hung up a large sign, on which was written: "I am the best tailor in the province."

When the second tailor saw this, he thought he would go one better, so he made a larger sign that read: "I am the best tailor in the whole country."

The third tailor thought: Am I supposed to say that I'm the best tailor in the whole world? He considered the matter for a very long time, and then put up a very small sign. It drew all the customers on the street to his shop, leaving the other two establishments deserted.

What did the third tailor's sign say? "I am the best tailor on this street."

He turned his eyes back to what was in front of him, starting out from the here and now. And this is why it was he who won the customers' approval.

To do one's own work well and to be a good, kind person is the first requirement of a junzi. But is just being a good, kind person enough to make you a junzi? Not quite.

To be a good person, with heart and mind in perfect equilibrium, is a necessary condition of being a *junzi*. But this is not enough on its own. For Confucius, the *junzi* is not only good, he must also be a great and noble person, always mindful of the affairs of the world, and he must have real drive and energy.

China's ancient history is peopled by the natural successors of Confucius: famous scholars and intellectuals who lived in times of desperate hardship and poverty, yet never forgot the ordinary people.

At a time when his tumbledown thatched cottage with its leaky roof was barely enough to shelter him, the poet and sage Du Fu: wrote: "How can I get a hundred thousand mansions, to shelter all the poor people of the world and bring smiles to their faces?" In other words, despite his own poor dwelling, he wanted everyone who was without a decent home to have one. Reading his words today, we feel that this is no idle boast on Du Fu's part. Instead we are moved by his generosity of spirit.

To give another example, the poet Fan Zhongyan believed that whether a *junzi* was "inhabiting the heights of the temples and halls of official life" or "situated amidst the far lakes and rivers," he should nevertheless feel concern both for the rulers of his country and for the common people of the world, and so "be the first to worry for the worries of the world, and the last to take joy in the joys of the world."

The influence of Confucius can clearly be seen in the poet's words.

At this point, you might begin to wonder if the Confucian idea that "the nation is my responsibility" must inevitably mean the sacrifice of one's own personal interests.

Actually, Confucius did not advocate such a sacrifice. On the contrary, his calm, warm, practical theory of human relations suggests that to do as much for society as your abilities allow is the greatest possible protection of the rights and benefits of all.

The Master said: "There are three things constantly on the lips of the gentleman, none of which I have succeeded in following: 'A man of benevolence never worries; a man of wisdom is never in two minds; a man of courage is never afraid.' Tzu-kung said: "What the Master has just quoted is a description of himself."

—ANALECTS XIV

However, Confucius believed that when seeking personal advantage you must not stray from the correct path, nor must you constantly seek shortcuts or petty victories. Confucius maintained that the difference between the *junzi* and the petty was whether they took the correct path or took shortcuts.

He said: "The *junzi* understands what is moral. The petty understands what is profitable" (*Analects* IV). The Chinese word *yi,* here translated as moral, sounds the same as another character, which means "appropriate" or "suitable." That is to say, the road that the *junzi* takes is the truest and most appropriate path from its beginning to its end. A petty individual, on the other hand, concentrates on personal advantage, and when pursuing that advantage it is very easy for them to fall into evil ways.

So how do the differences between a *junzi* and a petty person show themselves?

Confucius said: "While the *junzi* cherishes benign rule, the small man cherishes his native land. While the *junzi* cherishes a respect for the law, the small man cherishes generous treatment." In other words, a *junzi* does not have the same daily concerns as the petty person.

Not a day goes by without a *junzi* thinking about morality and self-cultivation, while a small-minded person considers only their own immediate circumstances—their home or their personal needs and desires. The *junzi* always live by the rules of a strict moral code, which cannot be broken, while petty people fill their heads with thoughts of trivial favors and how they can get the upper hand.

Someone who spends their days preoccupied with the affairs of their own family, such as how they can buy an apartment or climb the career ladder, who is full of little schemes to improve their family's lifestyle, is the kind of petty individual that Confucius was talking about. Of course there is nothing terribly wrong with this, but if someone allows their heart to become a prisoner as they scrabble for these scraps of personal advantage, if they discard the restraints of morality or the law in order to protect or expand such tiny advantages, then it can be very dangerous.

The *junzi* has always respected morality and the law. It's just like any one of us when we take the footbridge over a busy road, or wait for the lights at a pedestrian crossing: these acts may seem to be a restriction upon us, but these little restrictions, when they guarantee our safety, actually show mutual respect and enhance society.

Petty people, who are greedy for immediate gain, who use little loopholes and take small advantages, may get what they want once or twice, but there is a potential danger hidden there, and they're certain to come off the worse for it sooner or later. Let's take crossing the road again: as soon as a petty person sees the traffic lights are about to change, without waiting for the pedestrian signal, they rush across, thinking that by doing so they are getting someplace first, but we know very well what will happen sooner or later.

A petty person doesn't look at things in the right way, but is always eager to snatch small advantages.

In today's society, what can we do to become a *junzi*? We can start with the idea of "perseverance" or constancy. As young adults, we are all idealistic, full of ambition and hopes of achieving something useful. But why are these ambitions so often unfulfilled? In modern life we are faced with many complex choices, and with all this excitement and stimulation, it is hard for us to make decisions as we waver between a multitude of choices. We find it impossible to choose which path to take to achieve our ambitions. And this shows lack of "perseverance."

If we really persevere and learn to take the long view, even if we haven't reached the exalted state of those Confucius describes as having "no fixed abode but a fixed heart," being concerned more with what is inside us than with our external life, then we are well on the way to being a *junzi*.

There is a second standard for a *junzi*: "The *junzi* is conscious of his own superiority without being contentious, and comes together with other *junzi* without forming cliques" (*Analects* XV).

In other words, a *junzi* is sociable and gets on well with others. But nothing can undermine their inner dignity; they are never competitive with those around them. Neither would a *junzi* ever form cliques or scheme for personal advantage.

This is what Confucius means when he says: "The *junzi* agrees with others without being an echo" (*Analects* XIII).

In any large group of people, everybody's personal convictions will never be exactly the same, but a true *junzi* will listen earnestly as each person states their own point of view and will be able to understand and respect the logic of everyone's ideas, while at the same time holding fast to their own. This maintains both unity and harmony, while ensuring that everyone's voice is heard. These days, when we in China say that we want to build up a harmonious society, this means taking everybody's different voices and harmoniously blending them into the voice of the greater collective.

The Master said: "The gentleman agrees with others without being an echo. The small man echoes without being in agreement."

—ANALECTS *XIII*

Petty people are exactly the opposite, they "echo without being in agreement" (*Analects* XIII).

We have all come across situations at work, say, or at school or college, when an issue is being discussed and the boss or teacher says something. Before the words are properly out of their mouth, someone will immediately jump up and sycophantically say: "Yes, yes, my goodness yes, how right you are!" really laying it on with a trowel: "What a brilliant idea!" But as soon as the meeting or class is over, they turn to someone else and say: "What's that man going on about this time? I don't agree with him at all!"

Confucius gives another description of the ways in which the *junzi* and the petty behave very differently: "The *junzi* enters into associations but not cliques; the small man enters into cliques but not associations" (*Analects* II).

Junzi "enter into associations" with others who, like them, have high standards of morality and justice, which they use in their dealings with others, so they have many friends who cherish the same ideas and follow the same path. No matter how many friends a true *junzi* has, they will always be like oxygen in the air we breathe, making their friends feel happy and cared for. The Chinese character 比 for "enter into cliques" looks like two people standing close together. This means that petty people prefer to get together in their own little cliques; they don't like to be absorbed into the big collective.

For example, at a party a *junzi* will feel completely at ease with everyone there, whether old friends or strangers; but a petty person will skulk in a corner with their best friend, the two of them muttering away to each other, as thick as thieves.

Why are there such differences between people? Again, it is because the *junzi* and the petty do not exist in the same moral state. Confucius said: "The *junzi* is easy of mind, while the small man is always full of anxiety" (*Analects* VII). The reason why the petty are often found conspiring with others is that they have an uneasy conscience and want to plot for their own advantage and protect what they already have. When we talk about cronyism or forming cliques this is exactly what we mean. The mind of the *junzi,* on the other hand, is contented and composed, because he or she is in a state of peaceful ease without selfishness, and can be placid, and come together with others in a kind, friendly way.

In China, we have always regarded harmony as a thing of beauty, but what is true harmony? Confucius repeatedly shows us it is a tolerance toward others, a kind of melding and mingling, all the while maintaining different voices and different viewpoints. This is the way of the *junzi* in society.

Because there are so many differences between a *junzi* and a petty individual, you will find your dealings with them to be very different.

> *Confucius said: "The junzi is easy to serve but difficult to please. He will not be pleased unless you try to please him by following the Way, but when it comes to employing the services of others, he does so within the limits of their capacity. The small man is difficult to serve but easy to please. He will be pleased even though you try to please him by not following the Way, but when it comes to employing the services of others, he demands all-round perfection."*
>
> —ANALECTS *XIII*

Confucius explains these differences in a way that is extremely easy to understand, because he always puts the *junzi* and the petty side by side in order to compare them.

It is very easy to get along with a *junzi,* but you will find it very hard to ingratiate yourself with one. If you want to please them using underhanded means, they will not be at all pleased. They would never agree to wave you through ahead of others, or throw open the back door in exchange for small favors. But by the time they actually make use of you, they will have arranged a suitable place for you, based on your talents and abilities. This is what is meant by "within the limits of their capacity."

The defining characteristic of petty people is that it is very easy to suck up to them, but very hard to work alongside them. For example, if you do them a few small favors, or help them in some small way, even wine and dine them, this person will be very happy. Even if your way of pleasing them is not strictly moral, or even actually dishonest, they will still be very happy. But this kind of person is also rather difficult to work with. Don't ever think that once you've managed to get on their good side they will loyally smooth your path: even if you've put in a lot of effort, and spent a lot of money to buy them off, by the time they really want to employ someone, they will not arrange a job for you based on your talent and ability, but will demand perfection, and complain that you are not up to the mark here, haven't made the grade there, and all your efforts will have gone to waste. They will find ways to make things difficult for you, and put you in very awkward positions. Working with someone like this is very hard going.

Somebody once asked Zilu: "What kind of man is your teacher Confucius?" Zilu did not reply. Later, Confucius said to Zilu: "Why didn't you reply: 'He is the sort of man who forgets to eat when he tries to solve a problem that has been driving him to distraction, who is so full of joy that he forgets his worries and who does not notice the onset of old age'?"

This is in fact a portrait of Confucius, and also of the moral character that all Chinese intellectuals hoped to attain.

When it comes down to it, the aim of Confucian philosophy was to nurture those we might call followers of the Way of Confucius. In other words, its aim was to educate an elite class of scholar-officials whose primary mission was to serve their country and their culture.

In his poem "Memorial to Yueyang Tower," Fan Zhongyan describes the essence of this role: "Be the first to worry for the worries of the world, and the last to take joy in the joys of the world." For him, it means forgetting all about personal gains and losses, and absorbing yourself in the interests of the greater collective.

But once again we see that this profound conviction and sense of responsibility to society is founded on plain, simple things, and begins in the here and now. The starting point is in the cultivations of one's self, so that we become the best possible version of who we are.

That way, when, as often happens, we hear people complain that society is unfair, and that it is hard to deal with the world around us, rather than moaning about our fate or blaming other people, we do better to look inward and examine ourselves. If we can manage to fully understand where our limits lie, to be cautious and circumspect in our words and actions, to bring the spirit of Confucian courtesy and honor to the world, and to develop our mind and body, we will have many fewer things to trouble us, and so we will come to understand how to be a good person and how best to deal with the world.

I don't think such moral ambition is merely something to read about in the past. It is a way of living that every one of us can practice, now, in the twenty-first century, and we can begin today. That way, the happiness that Confucius and his disciples enjoyed can be a wellspring of happiness for us today. This is probably the greatest lesson that Confucius *can* give us, and his greatest gift.

If we have an optimistic and positive attitude, and a proper understanding of the boundaries and limitations of dealing with others, we can become the kind of person who brings happiness to others, and let our own happiness become a source of energy, shining like the sun on those around us, bringing comfort to our family and friends, and even, eventually, to the whole of society. But, as *junzi,* we must begin with our friends.

PART FOUR

The Way of Friendship

Of all the relationships we have, it is our friends who most directly reveal the kind of person we are.

If you want to understand someone, you only have to look at their circle of friends, which will tell you what their values and priorities are—after all, as is often shown, birds of a feather flock together.

But friends are divided into good and bad. The right sort of friend can help you a lot, but the bad sort will bring you a great deal of trouble, and may even lead you down the wrong road. Being able to choose your friends wisely is extremely important.

So what kind of friend is a good friend? What kind of friend is a bad friend? How can we make good friends?

Confucius attached a great deal of importance to the effect of friends on a person's development. He taught his own students to make good friends, and to avoid bad ones.

He said that there are three types of friends in this world who can help us.

The first are straight friends. *Straight* here means upright, honest, and fair-minded.

A straight friend is sincere and great-hearted; he or she has a kind of bright, transparent openness about them, without a trace of flattery. Their character will have a good influence on your own. They will give you courage when you are timid, and decisiveness and resolution when you are wavering.

The second are friends who are loyal and trustworthy.

This friend is honest and sincere in his or her dealings with others, and is never fake. Associating with this kind of friend makes us feel calm, composed, and safe; they purify and elevate our spirits.

The third is the well-informed friend. This kind of friend is possessed of a great deal of knowledge about a great many things and has seen a lot of the world.

The pre-Qin period (before 221 B.C.), when Confucius lived, was quite different from today, with our computers, Internet, sophisticated information resources, and all our different kinds of media. In those days, what did people do when they wanted to widen their outlook? The easiest way was to make a well-informed friend, absorbing the books he or she had read and all the friend's experience into their own direct experience.

When you find yourself dithering over a problem, unable to come to a decision, you would be well advised to go to see a well-informed friend. That friend's wide-ranging knowledge and experience will help you with your choice.

Having a well-informed friend is like owning a huge encyclopedia; we can learn many useful lessons from their experiences.

The three kinds of beneficial friends are true friends, loyal friends, and well-informed friends.

Confucius also said that there are three sorts of bad friends: "He stands to lose who makes friends with three other kinds of people." So what sort of people are these?

Confucius said that there are three kinds of bad friends, "the ingratiating in action, the pleasant in appearance, and the plausible in speech," and that to have these three types as friends is "to lose." So how can we tell what kind of people they are?

By the "ingratiating in action," Confucius meant flatterers and fawners—shameless toadies. We often encounter this sort of person in our lives. No matter what you say, they will always say: "That's just so brilliant." Whatever you do, they will always say: "That's amazing." They will never say "no" to you. On the contrary, they will slavishly follow you and take their tone from yours, praising you and paying you compliments.

This kind of friend has a talent for weighing your words and watching your expressions. They trim their sails to suit the wind, making sure they never do anything that they sense might displease you.

They are the absolute opposite to the good, straight friend. The hearts of these people are neither straightforward nor honest, and they have no sense of right and wrong. Their aim is to make you happy, but only so that they can get something out of it.

Most Chinese people have heard of the treacherous minister He Shen, a character in the TV series *Iron Teeth, Copper Teeth*. This man fawns on the Qianlong emperor in every possible way. He is the worst kind of sycophant and there's almost nothing he won't stoop to. He is a classic example of this type of bad friend.

A friend like this will make you feel unusually comfortable and happy, just like the Qianlong emperor in the TV series: he knew very well that He Shen was taking bribes and perverting the law, but even so he could not bear to be without him. As Confucius says, making friends with this kind of person is extremely dangerous!

Why?

After being told all the things you want to hear, and flattered into a state of contentment, it will start to go to your head; your ego will swell uncontrollably and you will become blindly self-important, caring for nobody but yourself. You will lose the most basic capacity for self-knowledge, and it will not be long before you bring down disaster on your own head.

This kind of friend is slow poison for the soul.

The second harmful friend is the person that Confucius called "the pleasant in appearance," or two-faced.

They will be all smiles and sweetness to your face, positively beaming as they dish out their compliments and flattery; they are precisely what Confucius meant by "a man with cunning words and an ingratiating face." But behind your back they will spread rumors and malicious slander.

We often hear people complain: "That friend of mine seemed so kind and loving, his speech was so gentle, his behavior so thoughtful, I believed he was my closest, most intimate friend, and I was genuinely committed to helping him. I poured out my heart to him, too; told him my innermost secrets. But he betrayed me, abusing my trust for his own ends; he started rumors about me, spread my secrets, destroyed my character. And then when I confronted him, he had the gall to deny it to my face, and put on a show of injured innocence."

This kind of person is false and hypocritical, the exact opposite of the frankness and honesty of the loyal and trustworthy friend.

People like this are the true "petty people"—petty, and with a dark shadow in their hearts.

However, such people often wear a mask of goodness. Because they have an ulterior motive, they will be very friendly toward you; they might be ten times nicer to you than somebody with no hidden agenda. So if you aren't careful and let yourself get used by this person, you will find that you have fitted shackles to your own wrists: this friend will not let you go unless you pay a heavy price. This is a test of our judgment, and of our understanding of people and the ways of the world.

The third kind Confucius called "the plausible in speech," referring to people who brag and exaggerate. Ordinary people might call them "fast talkers." There is nothing this kind of person doesn't know, and no argument they don't understand. They talk in an endless stream, carrying you along with their momentum until you can't help believing them. But in actual fact, apart from the gift of gab, they have nothing else at all.

There is a clear difference between this kind of person and "the well informed," which is that this kind of person has no real talent or knowledge. A person who is plausible in speech has a glib tongue, but nothing inside to back it up.

Confucius was always suspicious of glib people and their sweet words. A *junzi* should speak less and do more. Confucius believed that it is not what a person says that matters, but rather what they do.

Of course, in modern society there has been a change in attitudes and values: if people with real talent and true scholarship cannot communicate effectively and do not get their meaning across, it will obstruct their careers—and their lives.

However, if someone can only talk, and has no real skill, it is something far more harmful.

The three harmful friends found in The Analects of Confucius *are flattering friends, two-faced friends, and big-talking friends. On no account make friends with this sort of person, or else you will end up paying a painful price.*

But whether a person is good or bad is not written on their face. How can we make good friends and steer clear of bad friends?

If you want to make good friends, and avoid making bad, you need two things: the desire to make good friends, and the ability to do so. We have already seen how important "benevolence" and "wisdom" are, and they are key if we wish to make good friends. The desire to make good friends comes from benevolence and the ability to make them from wisdom. As you will remember, when Fan Chi asked his teacher what he meant by "benevolence," his teacher answered with only two words: "Loving people."

Fan Chi then asked, then what is this thing called wisdom?

The teacher replied, again with just two words: "Knowing people." To understand others is to be wise.

Plainly, if we want to make good friends, we must first have a kind, benevolent heart, be willing to get close to people, and have the desire to make friends; second, we must have the ability to discriminate. Only in this way can one make friends of real value. Once you have this basic standard, you will be well on your way to making friends of the very best kind.

In a sense, making a good friend is the beginning of a beautiful new chapter in our lives. Our friends are like a mirror: by watching them, we can see where we ourselves fall short.

However, there are some thoughtless people who spend almost all their time with their friends, but never seem able to make these comparisons.

Confucius said: "He stands to benefit who makes friends with three kinds of people. Equally, he stands to lose who makes friends with three other kinds of people. To make friends with the straight, the trustworthy, and the well informed is to benefit. To make friends with the ingratiating, the pleasant in appearance, and the plausible in speech is to lose."

—ANALECTS XVI

I'll give you a perfect example of someone who couldn't. The sixty-second volume of China's great history, *Records of the Grand Historian,* tells the story of Yanzi, the famous prime minister of the Kingdom of Qi.

As everyone in China knows, Yanzi was short and stumpy-limbed, with a plain, unremarkable face and rather coarse features. But he had a very handsome, tall, dashing charioteer.

This charioteer, funnily enough, thought that it was a very splendid thing to drive the chariot of the prime minister of the Kingdom of Qi. He was very proud of his position: every day sitting at the front of the chariot, whipping on the tall horses, while Yanzi had to sit behind in the covered part. He thought that his job as a charioteer was just the best thing ever!

One day, the charioteer came home to find his wife packing her bags, weeping bitterly. He asked in surprise: "What are you doing?" His wife replied: "I can't take any more, I'm leaving you. I'm ashamed to live with you."

The charioteer was astonished: "But don't you think I'm splendid?" His wife retorted: "What do you think splendid *is*? Look at Yan Ying, a talented man who's in charge of the whole country, yet he's so modest, sitting in the chariot without the least fuss or show. You're just a driver, but you think there's no end to your own splendor, strutting about with a high and mighty expression written all over your face! You spend all day with a man like Yan Ying, but you don't have the wit to learn anything at all from him to reflect on yourself—that's what has made me despair of you. Living with you is the most shameful thing in my life."

Eventually, Yan Ying heard about what had happened and said to his driver: "Since you have such a good wife, I should give you a better position." And he promoted the charioteer.

This story tells us that all the people around us, their ways of living and their attitudes in dealing with the world, can become a mirror for us. The key is to keep our wits about us.

The beneficial friends of whom Confucius approved are those who are useful to us. But by "useful" we do not mean to say that this friend will be able to help you get on in the world. On the contrary, Confucius never advocated taking up with rich or powerful people. Instead he favored making friends with people who can perfect your moral character, increase your self-cultivation, and enrich your inner self.

In classical Chinese there is a school of pastoral poetry. Poets of this school were notable for their desire to retreat from society, live in seclusion, and commune with the natural world, and their work praises the joys of nature and a simple, rural life.

So where can we find this communion with nature? It is not deep in the wild mountains and forests, but in real life. It has been said that "it is easier to find solitude in the marketplace than in the wilderness." Only a recluse who had not yet perfected his ability to cultivate himself would hide away up a mountain, and affectedly build a country retreat there; a true hermit has no need to retreat from the mundane world, but can live in the heart of a noisy, bustling city, doing things that are not the slightest bit different from everybody else, and differing from other people only in a certain inner calm and steadiness.

Everyone in China knows Tao Yuanming, one of the first recluses who, as we saw in Part One, would never compromise his ideals, and who became the founder of the pastoral school of poetry. Tao Yuanming lived in rather straitened circumstances, but he had a very happy life. The *Southern Histories* tell us that Tao Yuanming had no knowledge of music, but he owned a zither. This zither was just a big length of wood; it did not even have any strings. Every time he invited his friends to his house, he would stroke the piece of wood, saying that he was playing the zither, and he would pour all his heart into his playing, sometimes playing for hours until he was weeping audibly. And every time he did this, those friends who really understood music were also visibly moved. Tao Yuanming would play out the music of his soul on his stringless zither, while his friends drank wine and talked happily among themselves. Afterward, he would say: "I am drunk and I want to sleep. You may go." The friends left without making a fuss, and continued to meet on similar occasions in the future. Friends like this are true friends, because your souls share an unspoken understanding. And this kind of life is truly happy.

Make friends who are happy, and can take pleasure in their lives the way they are right now.

I once read an essay by the famous Taiwanese writer Lin Qingxuan, about a friend who asked him for a piece of calligraphy to hang in his study. The friend said to him: "Write me something that is extremely simple, but which will be helpful to me when I see it every day." Lin Qingxuan thought for a long time, and then wrote just four Chinese characters: "Think Often of One and Two." The friend did not understand, and asked what it meant. Lin Qingxuan said: "We all know the saying 'Out of every ten things in this world eight or nine will not go as I wish; and there is a mere handful of people I can communicate with.' Supposing we accept this, there will still be at least one or two things out of every ten that *do* go as we wish. I can't help you too much; all I can do is to tell you to think of those 'one or two' things, to turn your mind to happy things, to magnify the light of happiness, to keep the sadness in your heart at bay. As a friend, this is the best thing I can do for you."

There is a Western fable about a king who led a life of luxury and splendor, full of wine, women, music, and adventure; all the most beautiful and precious things in the world were his to command, but still he was not happy. Neither did he know what would make him happy, so he had his attendants summon his personal physician.

The doctor examined him for a long time, and then prescribed a cure: "Have your people search the kingdom for the happiest person in it. Wear his shirt, and it will make you happy."

So the king sent his ministers off to search for that person, and finally they found a genuinely happy man, incurably happy, in fact. But the ministers reported that they had been unable to bring back the man's shirt for the king to wear.

The king said: "How can that be? You have to bring me that shirt!"

The ministers said: "That man is a pauper and always goes about bare-chested—he doesn't even own a shirt."

This reminds us that in life true happiness is happiness of the soul, and does not necessarily have a very strong connection with external, material living conditions. Confucius lived in a time of considerable material poverty, and in his time the strength of true happiness came from a rich inner life, from behaving in the right way and from ambitions and desires, but also from good friends who learned from each other.

Having once come to understand what a good friend is, we also need to know how to get on well with them. Does having a good friend imply that we must be permanently joined together at the hip? In China, we often say of two people that they are so close they wear just one pair of trousers between them. But is this an appropriate closeness for friends?

Everything that lacks proportion or proper limits in this world will end up going too far, which, as we know, is as bad as not going far enough. Equally, when dealing with friends, we have to pay attention to boundaries. For example, when you make friends with a *junzi,* you need to know when to speak and when not to speak and to know how far you can reasonably go.

Confucius said: "When one is in attendance on a *junzi,* one is liable to three errors. To speak before being spoken to by the *junzi* is rash; not to speak when being spoken to by him is to be evasive; to speak without observing the expression on his face is to be blind" (*Analects* XVI).

Jumping up and stating your views before a conversation has had a chance to get anywhere is rash and insensitive, which is not a good thing. We all have our own particular interests, but you should wait until the time is ripe, when your chosen subject has become the focus of general attention and everyone is waiting to hear about it, and only then, and without undue haste, say your piece.

Many people now have their own blogs, or use websites in

which they eagerly display their innermost hearts for all to see. But in the past there were no such blogs, and everybody depended on the spoken word to understand one another and to communicate. When we get together with friends, there will always be a few people who go on and on about their own affairs: "I was out playing golf the other day," "I've just been promoted," and so on and so forth. Or when some women get together, there may be one who pushes herself forward to regale us with endless details of her husband and children. Of course, these are all things that she wants very much to say, but does everybody care about these things? That is to say, while she is the only one doing the talking, she strips away the rights of other people to choose a topic. To jump in with both feet and insist on saying your piece before the right time has come is certainly not good.

But there is another extreme: "not speaking when being spoken to." Confucius called this fault "being evasive."

In other words, the conversation has naturally reached a point where you should be the one to take the conversation further, but you drag your feet, and refuse to speak your mind. This kind of friend leaves everyone feeling excluded. Since the topic has already come this far, why don't you say anything? Is it self-protection? Are you deliberately holding yourself aloof? Or are you trying to whet our appetite? In short, keeping silent when you should speak is not good, either.

The third kind of situation is characterized by Confucius as "to speak without observing the expression on his face is to be blind," which is what we would today call an inability to read people.

"Blind" in this context is a great criticism. A person who gets up to speak without watching other people's expressions is a social illiterate. You must be careful to understand the person you are talking to; you should look to see what words can be said, and what is better left unsaid. This is the tactful respect that should always exist between friends.

And not just friends. There should be tactful avoidance of certain painful issues even between husband and wife, father and son. The life of every adult contains both private triumphs and private miseries. A true friend must not lightly touch on another's private pains, and for that you need to be able to read people. Of course, this is not a kind of slavish pandering to other people's tastes. Rather it creates a peaceful, friendly atmosphere for you and your friends, so that you can communicate freely.

There is a famous example of this.

The actress Vivien Leigh shot to fame with the Hollywood film *Gone with the Wind*, which won ten Oscars. This film was an immediate hit, and at the height of its fame she went on tour to Europe for the first time. Everywhere she went, thousands of journalists clustered eagerly around as Leigh's private plane touched down on the runway.

But one journalist, who lacked this ability to read people, pushed his way to the front and eagerly addressed a question to Leigh, who had just alighted: "Tell me, miss, what part did you play in this film?" At this question, Leigh turned on her heel, went back inside the plane, and refused to come out again.

Is asking a question like this in a situation you know nothing about so very different from being blind?

Apart from that, when offering friends advice, or giving them warnings, even if your intentions are good, you must be able to understand how far you can go.

Confucius said to Zigong that when giving advice, you must "advise them to the best of your ability and guide them properly, but stop when there is no hope of success. Do not ask to be snubbed" (*Analects* XII). That is, you don't necessarily have to be like a dose of bitter medicine; you don't have to smack them in the head and shout in their ear. It is perfectly possible for you to say what you have to in a pleasant but persuasive manner. This is "guiding them properly." If you can't get through to them, let it go at that. Don't wait until they lose patience with you, and don't go courting embarrassment.

Whatever you do, you can't just order people to do as you say. Today, not even mothers can expect that of their own children. Every individual is worthy of respect, and friends particularly must maintain mutual respect. Give them the right advice, or a proper warning; do your duty and no more. This is what good friends are for.

People make different friends in different stages of life. How do we make the friends that are best suited to us at each stage?

Confucius said that seventy or eighty years of human life seems to be a long time, but it can be divided into three distinct stages: youth, maturity, and old age. In every stage there are things that we need to be particularly careful about, which we sometimes call pitfalls. If you can manage to get past all three of these pitfalls, then you will encounter no other serious obstacles in your life. And to overcome these three sets of pitfalls, you can't do without the help of your friends.

Confucius said: "In youth, when the blood and *qi,* or life force, are still unsettled, he should guard against the attraction of feminine beauty." Young people are very prone to impulsive behavior, and they should make sure to avoid romantic difficulties. We often see high school and university students troubled by emotional problems. At this time of life, a good friend acts as an onlooker, who sees things more objectively and clearly, so they can offer solutions to the knotty problems we cannot untie ourselves.

When this pitfall is past, we arrive at middle age. Confucius said of this stage: "When the blood and *qi* have become unyielding, he should guard against bellicosity."

When people reach middle age, their family life is stable and they are established in their profession, so what is most on their mind at this time? The desire to make space for themselves, to expand their domain. However, this is all too liable to cause contradictions and conflicts with others, and both sides may very well come off worse as a result. So Confucius warns us that the most important thing for people in midlife is to take caution against getting involved in conflicts. Rather than fighting with other people, it is better to struggle with oneself, and try to find ways to improve. If, in the end, you miss out on that promotion, you should ask yourself whether it might not be because you could have done better in some way.

In this period, therefore, you should make friends with people who are calm and matter-of-fact. They will help you take the long view of temporary victories and defeats, overcome the temptations of material things, obtain spiritual comfort, and find a place of repose and respite for the soul.

But what should we beware of when we arrive in our later years? According to Confucius, "When the blood and *qi* have declined, he should guard against acquisitiveness."

In old age, people's minds show a tendency to slow down and become more tranquil. The philosopher Bertrand Russell compared this stage to a rapidly flowing river that rushes headlong through the mountains, but by the time it finally merges with the sea has become slow, broad, and placid. At this stage of life, people should have learned how to deal with possessions and achievements in a sensible way.

When young, we all live a life of addition, but after reaching a certain point, we have to learn to live by subtraction.

Rather than fighting with others, it is better to struggle with yourself, and try to find ways to improve yourself.

Society has given you friendship, money, human ties, and achievements, and by the time you reach old age you will have acquired a great many things, just like a house that gradually fills up with accumulated objects. If your heart becomes cluttered up with the things you have acquired, then they will end up holding you back.

What do our elderly friends discuss when they get together? A lot of the time, it involves grumbling. They complain that their sons and daughters have no time for them, saying: "I worked so hard to raise you—I did everything for you—wiped your bottom, changed your diapers!—but now you're busy, no time even for a quick visit." They grumble at the unfairness of society: "In my day we were busy making revolution, and all we got was a few dozen yuan a month—now look at my granddaughter, she went to a foreign company and was earning three or four thousand yuan straightaway. Is this fair to people like us who've worked our hearts out?"

If you keep saying things like this, then things that you should find pleasure in will become painful, a hidden burden dragging you down. At this time you need friends to help you come to terms with life, and learn how to let go of things, so that you can leave these annoyances and frustrations far behind you.

One thing we notice from a close reading of the *Analects* is that there are not actually many examples concerned with friendship alone, but that choosing friends is choosing a way of life. The kind of friends we make will first depend on our inner wisdom and self-cultivation; then on our particular circle of friends, and whether these friends are harmful or beneficial to our lives.

In short, once we have focused on our own heart and soul and on those who surround us, we must concern ourselves with what goals we should set ourselves as we move through life.

PART FIVE

The Way of Ambition

To be the best person we can be; to have a well-run family, to be of benefit to our country, to bring peace to the world: these are the things we should all aspire to.

When Confucius discussed ambition with his students he did not suggest that the higher your ambition the better. What really matters is that you are firm of purpose and keep true to your inner conviction.

Whether your goals are great or small, the basis for realizing them lies in finding the things that are closest to your heart. Allowing your heart to guide you will always be more important than chasing external achievements.

How should we understand ambition today? Is there a conflict between Confucius's attitudes and our modern goals?

Confucius said: "The Three Armies can be deprived of their commanding officer, but even a common man cannot be deprived of his purpose" (*Analects* IX). This is often quoted and it tells us that a person's goals are of the utmost importance, for they determine the development and direction of their whole life.

So when Confucius was teaching, he often made his students talk about their own ambitions. The ninth chapter of *The Analects of Confucius* contains one of the relatively few longer passages, which is called "Sitting in Attendance" and concerns a free and frank discussion between Confucius and his disciples on the subject of ambition.

One day, Confucius's four disciples Zilu, Zeng Dian, Ran Qiu, and Gongxi Chi were sitting with their master. Confucius spoke to them very informally, saying: "Because I'm a bit older than you, nobody wants to give me an official post. I often hear you say: 'Nobody understands my ambition!' Now, suppose there was someone who understood you, and planned to employ you. What would you do?"

Zilu had a hasty character. When he heard his teacher ask this, he instantly replied: "Give me a middle-sized kingdom with about a thousand war chariots, caught between two larger kingdoms, threatened with invasion from without and food shortages from within. If I am allowed to manage it, in less than three years I will inspire the entire population, and the common people will have come to know the meaning of morality."

We may feel that Zilu's ambition is pretty impressive, and one might think that a teacher like Confucius, who set so much store by ruling the country through his own principles of ritual and self-cultivation, would have been gratified to see one of his students achieve such a success, and save a nation from peril. Zilu didn't expect that Confucius's reaction would be not merely neutral, but even a little disdainful. "The Master smiled at him." He laughed briefly and coldly, without giving a direct response, and then went on to ask the second student: "Ran Qiu, what is your ambition?"

Ran Qiu's reply was noticeably more modest than Zilu's. He did not dare to mention so large a big state, or so many issues. "If there were a small state of sixty or seventy square leagues, or fifty to sixty square leagues, for me to govern, then after three years, I could give the common people enough food to eat and clothes to wear. As to enlightened government, rites, music, and philosophy, that will have to wait on a sage or a *junzi*." He meant that on a material level he could enrich the common people and give them all they needed, but as for belief in the nation, and bringing prosperity through ritual and music, that's beyond me, best to wait for a *junzi* who is wiser than me.

When he had finished, his teacher as before gave no direct response. Confucius then proceeded to ask the third student: "Gongxi Chi! What is your ambition?"

Gongxi Chi was a degree more modest still. He replied: "I do not say that I already have the ability, but I am ready to learn." First he stated his own attitude: I make no claims for myself, but since the teacher has asked me this, all I can say is that I am willing to learn. After that he said that he would like to dress in his robes of office and formal cap, to be a minor officiant in the official state rituals, or a minor functionary in meetings with foreign sovereigns and ministers. He did not mention ruling a nation or governing its people at all.

You will have noticed that each of these three students of Confucius was more modest than the last, each was more moderate than the last, each was closer to the starting point of his own life, and further from his ultimate aims.

In today's terms, the most important thing in a person's development is often not how high their ultimate ambition is, but the basis they have right now. We often have no shortage of great plans and aspirations, but we lack a practical road to lead us to our desires, one step at a time.

We do not lack grand, wide-ranging ambitions, but we lack a proper road to lead us there.

By this point only one person had not yet spoken, so Confucius asked: "Dian, how about you?"

Zeng Dian made no immediate reply. The language used here describes this moment remarkably vividly in just three characters, **鼓瑟希**, describing the sound of a burst of music that dies gradually away: up until that point his attention had been completely focused on a lute of fifty strings, which he was playing. When he heard the teacher ask him a question, he let the sound of the lute gradually fade, and then, with a final chord, he brought the melody to a close. Zeng Dian slowly and unhurriedly "put aside the lute and stood up." People sat on the ground in those days, and when students were listening to a teacher or holding a discussion, they would kneel, sitting back on their heels, but they had to stand up when replying to the teacher, to show respect. Zeng Dian put the lute aside, and then deferentially got to his feet and answered his teacher.

From these few words of description, we can see that Zeng Dian was a calm and collected type of person; he would not reply in a prompt, impetuous way like Zilu, but instead spoke pleasantly and persuasively, having thought everything through in advance. He first solicited the teacher's opinion, saying: "My ambition is not the same as my three classmates'. Am I allowed to talk about it?" The teacher said: "What does that matter? I just want every person here to talk about their ambition."

It was only then that Zeng Dian calmly began. He said: "My ambition is, at the end of spring, in the third month of the lunar calendar [April or May in the Western calendar], to put on newly made spring clothes, and in the season when all the world is in bloom and all of nature has come back to life, to go with a few adult friends, and a group of children, to bathe together in the waters of the River Yi, now free from the winter's ice. Once we are perfectly clean, we will bask in the spring breeze on the Rain Altar by the side of the River Yi, letting it blow into us and become one with us, to welcome the season of life and vitality along with the heavens and the earth, enjoying a rite of the spirit. When this rite is complete, everybody will happily return home, singing songs. This is all I want."

When Confucius heard this, he heaved a long sigh and said: "I am with Dian!" That is to say, Confucius's own ambition was the same as Zeng Dian's. These are the only words of judgment that Confucius uttered throughout the discussion.

When each man had described his ambition, the three students departed. Zeng Dian did not leave at once, but asked his teacher: "What is your opinion of what those three said?"

At first Confucius ingeniously deflected the question, replying: "They were just talking about their own ambitions, that's all."

But Zeng Dian then asked: "So why did you laugh when Zilu had finished his speech?"

Once this question had been asked, it was impossible not to reply. Confucius said: "It is by the rites that a state is administered, but in the way he spoke Zilu showed a lack of modesty. That is why I smiled at him. Courtesy is essential for governing a nation, but Zilu's words were entirely without modesty, so I laughed at him. What I meant was that if you want to govern a nation by means of courtesy and the rites, you must first have kindness, gentleness, and a kind of deference; this is the starting point. You saw how hastily Zilu replied, barging in to be first to speak. This shows that he lacked proper deference."

Following this Zeng Dian asked again: "But didn't Ran Qiu want to govern a nation? So why didn't you laugh at him?"

Confucius said: "But a state of fifty or sixty square leagues, or less, is still a state, surely?"

Zeng Dian asked again: "And wasn't Gongxi Chi talking about governing a nation as well? How come you didn't laugh at him?"

Confucius said: "If you have a temple, and meetings between rulers of the nations, if this isn't governing a country, then what is? If even someone as conversant with the Rites as Gongxi Chi says he wants to be a minor officiant, who is fit to be Master of Ceremonies?"

What Confucius meant was that he did not laugh at Zilu because he thought Zilu lacked the talent to run a state, but for the contents of his speech and his lack of modesty. The issue is not whether the area governed is big or small, or whether it is a kingdom; it concerns each student's attitude. Because Ran Qiu's and Gongxi Chi's attitudes were modest, and they had real ability, too, Confucius did not laugh at them.

As we have seen, Confucius had no time for those who make empty boasts. As he said: "It is rare, indeed, for a man with cunning words and an ingratiating face to be benevolent" (*Analects* I). He maintained that the true *junzi* should be "halting in speech but quick in action" (*Analects* IV): superficially, therefore, a *junzi* might not seem to be very impressive, but their inner heart is infinitely strong, resolute, and steadfast.

According to an ancient saying, there are three things that can never be taken back: a shot arrow, a spoken word, and a lost opportunity. Words once spoken are as hard to put back as water spilt from a jug, so a true *junzi* always gets the thing done first, then talks about it.

Confucius said: "The *junzi* is ashamed of his word outstripping his deed" (*Analects* XIV). In China we still talk about someone's "words outstripping his deeds" today. A *junzi* is ashamed for their words to go further than their actions.

A *junzi* does not talk about the things they want to do or the goals they want to achieve; a *junzi* always waits until they have done what they set out to do before casually dropping it into the conversation. This is what is meant by "he puts his words into action before allowing his words to follow his deeds" (*Analects* II).

There is another question here: Since Confucius did not disagree with Zilu's, Ran Qiu's, and Gongxi Chi's ambitions, why did he only give warm encouragement to Zeng Dian? What can we see from Confucius's support of Zeng Dian?

Zhu Xi, the great Song Dynasty scholar of Confucius, has a pretty authoritative reading of this discussion. He said Zeng Dian's ambition amounts to no more than "Remaining content with the place I am now in, taking joy in its daily business, I have no intention of sacrificing myself for the sake of others. . . ."

The Master said: "There is no point in seeking the views of a gentleman who, though he sets his heart on the Way, is ashamed of poor food and poor clothes."

—ANALECTS IV

Zeng Dian's life consisted of commonplace daily activities and he had no great wish to sacrifice himself for other people, but he did have a rich and full inner heart. To him, the perfection of his own character was an essential starting point, and his ambition was to see all of nature in its proper place. This means that his professional achievements would also be at a higher level than the other three, whose ambitions were purely professional.

This is what Confucius meant when he said "the *junzi* is not a vessel." A true *junzi* never tries to use professional achievements to get a better social position. On the contrary, the *junzi* inevitably sees self-cultivation as a starting point; you must want to begin with the things closest to you, and with perfection of the inner heart.

Confucius's strength is forever the strength of action, and not the strength of words.

In Confucius's view, the social responsibility of the *junzi* takes the form of idealism, which is a higher state than professionalism. *Junzi* have never been confined to a particular profession. As he said: "The *junzi* is not a vessel" (*Analects* II). A vessel in this context means someone who reaches the desired standard and conforms to the rules, doing the job demanded of them but no more.

We must always remember that human beings are strange creatures; our thoughts determine our actions, which is to say, as we have seen, that our attitude determines everything. The things that each of us do in society every day are generally similar, but we all have a different explanation for them.

I once read a book by a fifteenth-century religious reformer, who tells a story from when he was young. This experience would change his entire life.

He wrote that one day he walked past a huge building site in the blistering sun, full of men carrying bricks, all streaming with sweat.

He went to ask the first man: "What are you doing?"

That man said, in a very surly manner: "Can't you see? It's hard labor—carrying bricks!"

The writer tried his question on a second person. This man's attitude was a lot more placid than the first: he stacked the bricks he was carrying into a neat pile, ran his eyes over them, and then he said: "I'm building a wall."

After that he went to ask a third person. There was a sort of cheerful, kindly glow to the man as he put down the bricks he was carrying, raised his head, wiping away the sweat, and said very proudly: "Are you asking me? We're building a *church.*"

We can see that the things these three people were doing were identical in every way, but their explanations were entirely different.

The first man's attitude I call pessimism. He regarded everything we do as just another burden in a life of toil, focusing on the hardship of the moment (which of course really does exist).

The second man's attitude is what I call professionalism. He knew that he was building a wall, that this wall was part of a completed product, and that he had to do his best and earn his wages. It was his professional duty, and his attitude is well up to the standard for professionalism. This is the state that Confucius called "being a vessel," and as a vessel he was more than adequate. But he did not have any higher calling.

The third kind of attitude I call the idealist attitude. That is to say, he sees every brick in front of him at that moment, and every drop of sweat, and he knows that all this is leading to the creation of a sacred place, a church. He knows that every step he takes is of value, and he knows what the final result of all his hard work will be. At this time, he works as more than just a vessel. The things he does are connected to our life, to our dreams, to whether we can finally build a church. And at the same time, because he is immersed in the dream of a church, he goes beyond individual success to achieve something much greater.

A *junzi*'s role in society adapts to the context, and moves with the times. It is not a *junzi*'s actions that are important, but the motives behind those actions. The *junzi* are the conscience of a society. But being a *junzi* is something that everybody can achieve. That dream, that goal, is both high and far-reaching, but it is not beyond our reach. In fact it exists in the here and now, in the inner hearts of each one of us.

Every one of us has our own goals, but in the hurried, endlessly repeating cycles and rhythms of work, how much time and space do we have to pay attention to our inner heart? The part of ourselves that performs in a social role is plainly visible, but often we muffle the voice of our own spirit.

I once read a short story about a man who was very unhappy with his life. He suspected it might be the early symptoms of depression, so he went to see a psychiatrist.

He said to the doctor: "Every day I am terribly afraid of going home from work. When I'm working, everything is normal, but as soon as I get back home I feel full of doubts and fears. I don't know what my heart's true ambition is; I don't know what choices I should make. The closer it gets to evening, the worse this feeling of dread becomes, and the pressure gets more and more intense. I often can't sleep a wink all night. But the next day when I go to work in the morning, and enter into my professional role, my symptoms disappear. If this carries on for much longer, I'm afraid I'll go mad."

When the doctor had heard him out, he made a suggestion: "There's a famous comedian in our city; he's a fantastic performer. Everyone who sees him splits their sides laughing, and forgets all their troubles. To start with, why don't you try going to one of his shows? After that we can have another talk, to see whether it's done anything to help you. Then we'll discuss a plan of action."

When he had heard this, the man did not speak for a long time. When he finally raised his face to look at the doctor, it was dripping with tears. Almost too overcome to speak, he said: "I am that comedian."

Success in our professional life is not necessarily the heart's true ambition.

This is just a fable, but it is the kind of thing that can very easily happen in our lives today. Think about it: when a person has become accustomed to a role, and cheerfully performs within that role, believing it to be his or her ambition, and a sign of professional success, how much room is left for spiritual longings? How much space have we left outside our roles, for us to truly know our own hearts? This is at the root of the panic and disorientation many people experience when they step outside their professional roles.

There is another interesting little story:

There once were three little field mice running about between the fields, all busy with their preparations to get through the winter.

The first field mouse was searching furiously for provisions, carrying all kinds of grain and seeds into his burrow.

The second field mouse was searching for things to keep out the cold, and he dragged a lot of straw and fluffy seed heads into the hole.

And the third field mouse? He kept wandering about the fields, looking at the sky, then at the earth, and then lying down to rest for a while.

His two hardworking companions rebuked the third mouse as they toiled away, saying: "You're so lazy, making no preparations to get through the winter. Let's see how you manage when winter comes!"

The third field mouse made no attempt to explain himself.

Later, when winter arrived, the three field mice hid themselves away in a cramped little burrow. They had no shortage of food and had everything they needed to keep out the cold, but they had nothing to get on with all day. Gradually, boredom set in, and they had no idea how to pass the time.

Things that on the surface appear to be completely valueless can in fact be a starting point for us to bring calm and stability to the inner heart.

So the third field mouse started to tell stories to the other two: about how he met a child on the edge of the field one autumn afternoon, and what he saw the child doing; about a man he saw by the pond one autumn morning, and what he was doing. He told them about conversations he had, and a song he had heard from a bird . . .

It was only then that his two companions realized that this field mouse had been collecting sunshine to get them through the winter.

If we look again at Zeng Dian's ambition now—to hold a rite to cleanse himself and get close to nature, in the season when the earth has thrown off the shackles of winter and all of nature is rejoicing—it appears to have no practical significance whatever, but such rituals can bring peace and order to the inner heart. To enjoy such peace and order, we must be as one with the heavens and the earth, able to keenly perceive the changes in nature's rhythms, and to experience the four seasons, and the natural landscape of mountains and rivers, the wind and the moon.

To us today, this is a great luxury. In our modern world, there are too many things that are out of season: in the heat of summer, our homes have air-conditioning to waft us with cool breezes; when the cold winter comes, central heating makes the house as warm as spring; at Chinese New Year at the end of winter, the table is loaded with brightly colored vegetables, grown in plastic greenhouses. When life grows oversimplified like this, the traces left in our lives by the four passing seasons become blurred; seasonal changes and the annual patterns of nature can no longer arouse any reaction in our hearts. We lack Zeng Dian's sensitivity—sensitivity that made him wish, at the height of spring, to let himself be shaped by it—and thereby lack this platform from which we can let our larger ambitions take wing and fly.

The relationship between our goals and our actions is just like that of a kite and a string. The key to how far a kite can fly is in the string in your hands. And this string is the aspirations of your inner heart. The more calm, matter-of-fact, and steady your mind, the easier you will find it to reject grandiose, showy external things and respectfully listen to the tranquil voice of your inner heart. This means that when you take up a role in society, you will not lose touch with yourself; you will be able to bear your responsibilities cheerfully, and to achieve the very best.

Many people feel that the ambitions described in "Sitting in Attendance" differ somewhat from our usual understanding of what Confucius and his students had to say on the subject of ambition. For example, contrary to what Zengzi says at another point, these ambitions are not heavy: "A gentleman must be strong and resolute, for his burden is heavy and the road is long" (*Analects* VIII).

But if we stop and think about it for a moment, the attitudes described in "Sitting in Attendance" are in fact the trees on which those "burdens," those great personal and social ambitions, will grow and bear fruit. If, in their professional role, a person lacks this sense of calm, or an understanding of his or her inner heart, they will only be good for giving orders, and have no hope of improving themselves.

The key to remember is that this self-improvement is not selfish. Confucius's emphasis on the cultivation of our inner heart in no way suggests that we should relinquish our responsibility to society; rather we cultivate ourselves so that we can better serve society.

In China, there is a type of person, the *shi,* who are the highest intellectual class, people who see the society in which they live as their own responsibility. It is a very honorable status sometimes referred to as that of a "gentleman-scholar."

Confucius once said: "A *shi* who is attached to a settled home is not worthy of being a shi" (*Analects* XIV). In other words, if someone spends their days with no room in their head for anything but their own small family circle, and their own mundane, day-to-day affairs, then they cannot become a true *shi*.

It is just this aspect of responsibility that Confucius's student Zigong touched upon when he asked Confucius: "What must a man be like before he can be said truly to be a *shi*?"

His teacher told him: "A man who can control himself and who, when sent abroad, does not disgrace the commission of his lord can be said to be a *shi*."

What Confucius meant was that people must understand courtesy and integrity; they must be able to control their behavior; they must have a firm, steadfast heart and will not compromise their standards. But at the same time they must be useful to society—that is, they must work for the good of society. In other words, once a person has achieved this inner cultivation, they will not allow themselves to become complacent; they will continue to go out and do useful things; they will be loyal to their mission, and "not disgrace the commission of their lord." This is, according to Confucius, the highest standard for the *shi*. And it is not easy, because there is no way of knowing in advance what your mission might be.

Zigong thought this standard was too high, so he asked: "May I ask about the grade below?" Is there another standard that's a bit lower?

Confucius replied: "Someone praised for being a good son in his clan and for being a respectful young man in the village." In other words, someone praised by their extended family for being good to their parents, and popular in their village for the respectful behavior shown toward fellow villagers. If you can start from what is around you, if you can shine with the light of human love and human ties and use the strength of this love to win the approval of those around you, and not shame your ancestors, this is the second level of *shi*.

Zigong asked again: "And the next?" Is there another, lower level?

Confucius said: "A man who insists on keeping his word and seeing his actions through to the end could, perhaps, come next, even though he sometimes shows a stubborn petty-mindedness."

Modern readers will probably be flabbergasted by this. Such high standards of behavior only let you into the third class of *shi*? A person who insists on keeping his or her word and seeing their actions through to the end, and who, having once agreed to do something, will get it done, regardless of the methods used, and regardless of the consequences, and who always keeps their promises—all this, and this person can only at a pinch be classed as a third-class *shi*? How many people today can actually manage to insist on keeping their word and seeing their actions through to the end?

Although they are difficult to achieve, these three standards are, according to Confucius, what define the sort of mature individual who can successfully take on any position in society.

There is a story about Lin Xiangru, the famous minister of the Kingdom of Zhao during the Period of the Warring States (475–221 B.C.), which helps to demonstrate the highest standard of *shi:* the person who "does not disgrace the commission of his lord."

It happened that the King of Zhao acquired the Hesheng Jade, a jewel of incalculable rarity and value, worth more than many cities. The King of Qin was eager to get his hands on it, so he sent an ambassador to the King of Zhao, saying that he was prepared to exchange fifteen of his cities for this piece of jade. The King of Zhao knew that Qin was a ruthless and greedy kingdom: once the piece of jade reached Qin it would be impossible to get it back. But Lin Xiangru said: "If we don't take the jade, we will put ourselves in the wrong. I'll take the jewel and if I can't get the fifteen cities that were promised, I will lay down my life rather than let it fall into the hands of the King of Qin. So, as long as you have me, you have the jade."

When Lin Xiangru arrived in the Kingdom of Qin bearing the Hesheng Jade, the King of Qin received him casually in a side hall, and allowed his ministers and the ladies of the court to pass the priceless treasure around, sniggering among themselves. When Lin Xiangru saw this, he realized that the Kingdom of Zhao was being treated with the same lack of respect as the Jade. However, getting the jewel back would be no easy task. So he said to the King of Qin: "Your Majesty, this jade has a flaw; give it to me and I will show you." When the King of Qin returned that piece of jade into his hands, Lin Xiangru retreated several paces, backing up against a pillar. He stood there and clutched the stone and, in a towering rage, he said to the King of Qin: "When you received our treasure in such a place as this, you dishonored both this jade and the Kingdom of Zhao. Before we came, we burned incense, made sacrifices, and fasted for fifteen days, as a mark of respect to the Kingdom of Qin. I came here reverently bearing the jade, but you casually handed it over to your ministers and court beauties. I can see from your cavalier attitude that you have no real intention of giving us fifteen cities in exchange. If you really want it, you should fast and burn incense for fifteen days as we did, and hand over those fifteen cities and then I will return the jade to you. If you don't do this, I will shatter both my head and this piece of jade at the same instant on the great pillar of your Golden Hall." The King of Qin was afraid and hurriedly agreed to his demands.

Lin Xiangru knew that the King of Qin would not keep his word, and so he ordered his family to flee overnight back to Zhao, taking the treasure with them. He, however, remained behind, and confessed what he had done to the King of Qin. He said: "I know that you have no real intention of giving us those cities, but by now the jade has already been returned intact to Zhao."

Stories of this kind are not uncommon in the ancient books and records of classical China. The way in which someone approaches a professional task when everything around them suddenly changes is a good test of that person's maturity. How can a person conquer their fear; how can they remain calm, collected, and unflustered? For this we need to find something on which we can rest our hopes. It may not necessarily be something commonly viewed as a great ambition: power, money, or anything of that sort. It could be said that each of us in the great circle of life has one goal that they care about more than anything else. And anyone who can find such an ideal on which to pin their hopes will have an anchor for their whole life and a firm foundation for their inner heart.

For Confucius, all great goals are built upon such plain and simple foundations. Positive thinking is one of the most powerful forces in the world and what we all crave is time for reflection—not material luxury, but the luxury of a spiritual journey.

Confucius once said that he wanted to go to live in the remote eastern region of China populated by non-Han Chinese, and known at that time as the land of the Nine Barbarian Tribes.

Somebody tried to talk him out of it, saying: "But could you put up with their uncouth ways?" Could you stand to live in such a poor, backward place?

Confucius replied simply: "Once a *junzi* settles among them, what uncouthness will there be?"

There are two interpretations of his reply. The first is that the *junzi*'s "mission" is to the whole world; to the *junzi* a place is no more than an external environment, whether it is rich and luxurious, or simple and crude. Secondly, the mind of a *junzi* has a constant, stable energy, which can make the things around them light up and burst into flower. The atmosphere they create around themselves and within their own life can transform even a backward, uncouth place.

In China we have a very well-known poem written in the Tang Dynasty called "On My Humble House," by Liu Yuxi, who demonstrates the response of all China's gentleman-scholars throughout the ages to life in humble surroundings. He said that we might not be able to change the material environment we live in, but there is no need to be too exacting in our demands, for it is the people around us who create our most important environment. He spoke of "the laughter of the cultured and wise," describing how "no vulgarity may enter in." In other words, a person's home may be poor and ramshackle, but it is the place in which they and their friends discuss their dreams and ambitions. And therefore their humble living conditions are not what really matters.

How, then, should we reach our goal? We should take a simple, commonplace starting point, which will lead us to spiritual happiness.

The Way of ambition will give us a fixed, accessible starting point, and a resource and storehouse of inner happiness.

When we really understand "Sitting in Attendance"; when we have read those heartfelt words "I am with Dian"; when we know that such a sage, an example for all of us throughout the ages, wished for a life of "bathing in the River Yi, and enjoying the breeze on the Rain Altar," and wanted in the late spring to "go home chanting poetry," we will see that his desire is in fact very similar to that solitary communion with the spirits of heaven and earth described by the philosopher Zhuangzi.

In other words, the ancient sages and men of virtue all started out on their spiritual journey from a fixed core: their own personal values. First they came to understand the yearnings of their own spirit, and only then could they make great plans or form grand ambitions.

We all want to find the fixed points in our lives, so that we, too, can find a starting point for the long journey ahead of us. Let us build a wisdom of the soul, founded on the wisdom that comes from self-knowledge; let us enter into the wisdom of Confucius, so that we too can be his peaceful students, overcoming the changes and turmoil of the ages to see his serene, steady, peaceful face today. Let us remember his encouragement to get close to nature, and, in the rare intervals in our crowded, busy lives, treat ourselves to a small, private rite of the soul, unlike that comedian whose personality was split, and who no longer dared to face his inner heart. In fact, in our modern era, the serenity we find in Confucius's everyday concepts, the clarity and truth of his ideas, and the strength we find within them should encourage us to cherish our inner hearts, and recognize that the roots of all of our ambitions and goals are found deep within us.

Confucius never forgot how difficult this was. But his teachings guide us through the different challenges we face as we grow older. He helps us understand what is required of us at every stage on our journey through life.

PART SIX

The Way of Being

Confucius described his life as having six stages.

His description of his journey through life still has a great deal of significance for us in the modern world.

The key is recognizing what he wants us to draw from this wisdom to make our lives more effective and of greater value.

Throughout history, people have lamented the passing of time more than anything else.

Everyone in China also knows the couplet written by Sun Ran for the twin pillars of the Daguan Pavilion in Kunming. The first line says: "The five hundred *li* of Lake Dianchi spread out before your eyes." The second: "Thousands of years of things past come at once to mind."

To a philosopher, the surging, flowing waters of a river are not only a natural phenomenon. Another thing that flows away like the waters of a river and can never be held back or returned to the way it was is time.

In his poem "Lament by the River," the poet Du Fu wrote: "I weep for my past life, and tears soak my garments. The river waters roll by, unchanging and without end." And in "Contemplating the Past on Mount Xisai," Liu Yuxi said: "In our human life, how many sources there are of grief and regret! The mountains stand unchanging, as the cold winter river flows between them." Human life is but a short span, while nature is eternal; the powerful contrast is enough to jolt the spirit and bring tears of sorrow to our eyes.

It is no wonder that that Tang Dynasty poet Zhang Ruoxu posed this eternal question to the moon in "Moonlight Night on the River":

Who was the first man to see the moon on the riverbank? In what year did the moon first shine on man? Human lives ceaselessly come and go, generation after generation, but the river and the moon remain constant year after year. I don't know who the river and the moon are waiting for; I only see the waters of the Yangtze flowing away.

Confucius was no exception. "While standing by a river, Confucius said: 'What passes away is, perhaps, like this.'" Everybody in China knows these words. It is an obscure phrase, only just hinting at its meaning, but it carries within it a deep regret at the changes and hardships of human life.

In the midst of this vast, endless universe, amid the unending cycles of nature, each human life is so tiny and insignificant, passing in the blink of an eye. So how should we plan our brief lives?

At the same time that Confucius was sighing over the water as it flowed past, he described to his students, and to thousands of generations after them, a path through life.

At fifteen I set my heart on learning; at thirty I took my stand; at forty I came to be free from doubts; at fifty I understood the Decree of Heaven; at sixty my ear was attuned; at seventy I followed my heart's desire without overstepping the line.

—ANALECTS *II*

This is a rough set of coordinates for human life, in which several stages are particularly emphasized. Let's take a quick look at the path through life that the sage describes for us, to see what lessons we can draw from it, and what it means to us today.

A human life is no more than a brief moment borrowed from time; as the months and years flow past, we take these few brief years and carve them into a certain shape, hoping to create something eternal, to be our memorial once we are gone.

As we have seen, we all have ambitions and things that motivate us, but we have to begin by coming to terms with the society we live in. Study begins with the transformation of a natural, unformed human being into a person shaped by the rules of society. When Confucius says "At fifteen I set my heart on learning," he is describing his own starting point on that journey, and it was also what he required of his students.

Confucius himself often said: "I was not born with knowledge but, being fond of antiquity, I am quick to seek it" (*Analects* VII). Even Confucius was not born understanding everything. But because he was deeply interested in the culture and the experiences of the ancients, he was able to work tirelessly and study diligently.

Today we want to build a society where education is freely available to all. But what kind of learning is good learning?

In today's age of information there are just too many things to learn. Today's children no longer wait until fifteen to "set the heart on learning"; many start learning before they are even five years old. But what do they actually learn? A few children memorize the values of π to many places after the decimal point; others can recite long poems in classical Chinese as a party piece for guests. But will these things really be useful for the rest of their lives? How many of today's "inclinations to learning" are what Confucius spoke of as "studying in order to improve oneself"? And how many are studying in order to make use of what they have learned?

While standing by a river, the Master said: "What passes away is, perhaps, like this."

—ANALECTS *IX*

In the modern age, the most distressing thing for us is that there is too much information; our biggest difficulty is that of choice. We desperately need a well-laid-out plan to guide us through the maze of choice so that we can learn what we really need to learn.

Confucius's attitude was always that going to "excess is worse than not far enough." The best things all have degree; if you are greedy you will bite off more than you can chew, and your brain will become like the hard drive of a computer, full of passive knowledge that is not doing anything. You would do better to make use of your limited knowledge and study in order to master just one subject, to absorb it into your life.

Confucius said: "If one learns from others but does not think, one will be bewildered. If, on the other hand, one thinks but does not learn from others, one will be in peril" (*Analects* II). We must learn, think, and make use of what we have learned, all at the same time.

In China our present college education system hands out knowledge in standardized lengths, but we can add more breadth to it. Confucius's preferred method of learning, in which thinking and learning are combined, has a lot to teach us.

Through study, experience, and training, we will gradually advance, coming to understand things both intellectually and intuitively. This will be the state we are in as thirty approaches.

"At thirty I took my stand."

In China, "taking one's stand at thirty" is still a phrase that you will very often hear. At this age, just about everybody begins to look inside themselves, asking: "Have I taken my stand?"

So what is taking one's stand? Do you have to have a car, an apartment, or some professional position before you can be said to have taken your stand? And how does reaching the age of thirty, which in China we call the year of taking a stand, affect us?

These days, we seem to reach adulthood later and later, especially in the big cities, where thirty-year-olds still get called "boys" and "girls." So how are we to judge whether a person has "taken their stand" in the world? And what responsibilities does taking a stand entail?

For example, when children have just started at primary school, they believe that the sun is bright, flowers are a beautiful bright red, people's hearts are good, that the world is full of tender feelings, that the prince and the princess will come together in the end, and that there is no sorrow or distress in life.

The Master said, "The Wise find joy in water; the benevolent find joy in mountains. The Wise are active; the benevolent are still. The Wise are joyful; the benevolent are long-lived."

—ANALECTS VI

But once they reach their teenage years, a powerful tendency to rebel will emerge, and in their twenties, when they have just entered adult society, they will feel that nothing in the world is the way it should be, that the adult world has cheated them, that life is full of ugliness, wretchedness, and deceit. These are the "angry young men" that we often hear about. This part of growing up has its own special bleakness, which is an inevitable reaction to the first stage. But by the time we hit thirty, we should be at the stage of fulfillment, which means neither thinking that everything in front of you is bright and sunny, as a ten-year-old would, nor that everything is bleak and cruel, as people in their twenties would.

Taking a stand at thirty is first and foremost an inner stand; finding your place within society comes afterward.

From the point of view of inner spiritual independence, truly good learning means applying all that we have learned to ourselves, so that the things we have learned become our own. This is the kind of study that China's culture demands of us.

So the period from fifteen to thirty is about the process of learning. But how is one to arrive at this integrated state, where all that we have learned becomes our own?

Chinese people traditionally approach learning in two ways:

one we call "I explain the Six Classics," the other "the Six Classics explain me."

The first method requires a lifelong study of the classics, lasting well into old age; by the time your hair is white and you have finished reading all the books, you will be fit to make commentaries on the classics.

But the second method, "the Six Classics explain me," is on an altogether higher plane. It involves using the spirit of the Classics to explain and inform your own life.

Thirty is the age at which to build up inner self-confidence. This self-confidence is not set up in opposition to external things. Rather it creates a kind of harmony, in which both internal and external are lifted up. This is like the couplet on Mount Tai: "The sea reaches out to its farthest extreme, the sky is a shore: On ascending the summit, I will be another peak of the mountain." This is one of the ways in which the Chinese relate to mountains and rivers. Our aim is not to conquer or subjugate them; instead the mountains and rivers are seen as elevating us. Just as the sea stretches away endlessly, with no shore but the sky, making it seem as if the whole world is stretched out before us, on reaching the topmost pinnacle of a mountain it is not so much that I am trampling the high mountain beneath my feet, but that the mountain peak on which I stand has raised me to new heights.

This is the state that we call "the Six Classics explain me."

Confucius always taught his students to live plainly and simply: do what is in front of you as well as you can; there's no need to worry about most things, so don't worry about them.

For example, it is well-known that "the topics Confucius did not speak of were prodigies, force, disorder, and gods" (*Analects* VII). Confucius did not like to talk about things like gods and spirits, because his attention was focused on real, tangible behavior.

When Zilu asked him once about ghosts and spirits, Confucius said calmly: "You are not able even to serve man. How can you serve the spirits?" You can't even get living people's business straight in your head; how can you think of going to honor dead people? That is to say, before you start to study you should keep things simple, beginning with what is in front of you. Don't immediately go pondering empty, profound things.

Zilu was not ready to give up, and said: "May I ask about death?"

Again, Confucius said serenely: "You do not even understand life. How can you understand death?"

This still has such a lot to teach us today. When studying, first do your very best to understand the things in life that are within your reach. Do not overstretch yourself to ponder things that are beyond you or deeply profound. Until we reach the age of taking one's stand, it is only through learning a little bit at a time that we can truly stand up.

For me, then, "taking one's stand at thirty" is not a means of evaluating whether you have measured up to any external social standards. Rather it is a way of evaluating your life against internal standards, of the heart and the soul, in order to establish whether you have begun to acquire bright, calm, unhurried introspection, and therefore whether you have reached a state where you can deal confidently and decisively with your own affairs.

Going beyond material gain and focusing on what is within, is, for me, the greatest proof that one has taken one's stand.

There are many examples of this attitude in Chinese culture. Take the old man in the straw rain hat in Liu Zongyuan's poem. He is "fishing alone in the snowy winter river" in the bitter cold, dangling his hook for nothing but its own sake. Or take the great poet and scholar Wang Huizhi's journey in a small boat on a snowy night to visit his friend Dai Kui: when he came to his friend's door he turned and left without bothering to knock. Why? Because he had come on an impulse, missing his friend; when he reached his friend's door the impulse vanished, and he went home. These ancients were loyal to their own souls; the direction shown to them by their heart determined the direction of their actions.

Between thirty and forty, people move on from the years of "taking one's stand" to what Confucius called the years of "freedom from doubts."

These should be the best years of our lives.

But can everybody achieve "freedom from doubts" by the age of forty?

In our modern society, people in their forties have reached the middle years of life. They are known and respected in their chosen profession, but they have an older generation above them, a younger generation below, and this puts great pressure on them. In such a testing situation, what is the best way to keep our hearts free from doubts and anxiety?

Confucius frequently elaborates on the idea of "freedom from doubts." How can a person truly achieve freedom from doubts and fears? It requires great wisdom.

The years from taking one's stand to freedom from doubts are the best time of our life. Before the age of thirty, people live by addition, constantly acquiring the things they need from the world: experience, wealth, relationships, reputation, and so on. But the more material things we have, the more perplexed and doubtful we become.

After thirty, we have to start learning to live by subtraction—you must learn to let go of the things that are not what your soul really needs.

Our heart is like a new house: when its owners have just moved in, they want to fill it up with furniture, curtains, and other decorations. As a result, the house ends up as cluttered as a narrow Beijing alley, full of odds and ends, and we have nowhere left to put ourselves. We become enslaved by our possessions.

Learning to live by subtraction means shedding the people we do not want to be our friends, refusing to do the things we do not want to do, and turning down the money that we do not want to earn. Only when we dare to let go, and know how to let go, can we truly free ourselves from doubts.

So what is freedom from doubts? It is when a person can think and act according to the ideas explored in *The Doctrine of the Mean*.

The Doctrine of the Mean is one of the *Four Books* that became the core texts of Confucian learning and helped define the highest standards of behavior in ancient China. Philosophically speaking, it concerns the most appropriate "degree" to which a thing is done. Often nowadays it is mistakenly understood to imply mediocrity, slyness, and low cunning; the Doctrine of the Mean is widely seen as representing compromise at the expense of principle, perhaps even a blurring of the line between right and wrong.

The Doctrine of the Mean says: "When happiness, anger, grief, and joy are not expressed, this is called the Mean; when they do find expression, but in a restrained and balanced way, this is called Harmony. The Mean is the great root of the world, Harmony is the great Way of the world." That is to say, the ideal state is one where everything is in harmony, with heaven, earth, and all of nature each safely in its own place. This attitude means that even if the outside world treats you unfairly, you now know where you stand, and knowing this will help you to cope with the blows and regrets that life metes out and will give you a foothold in life.

When it comes to judging the best ways of doing things, if one does not care which method is correct, and concentrates only on which method is most appropriate, the most appropriate way almost never involves going to extremes.

The great philosopher Feng Youlan once said: "Learn from the dynasties of old to help the new order; our ideals should be the very highest, but our actions should follow the Way of the Mean." The Way of the Mean actually entails reaching a very high moral state by the most appropriate method. As the Chinese ancients said: "At their extremes, glory and radiance return to the Middle Way." In your twenties and thirties you forge your way ahead through life, but it is not until you have reached forty, the years of freedom from doubts, that you can show tranquil levelheadedness and a sense of responsibility. And when someone has reached this stage, a change will take place in many of that person's standards.

Then, when another ten years have passed, and we reach fifty, more changes will have taken place.

At fifty, Confucius said that he "understood the will of Heaven." What did he mean? Is it what we mean when we say: "If a thing is fated it will happen sooner or later; if a thing is not fated to be, don't try to force it"? Does it mean that when we reach fifty we must resign ourselves to our fate?

If we want to answer this question, we must first of all be clear on what exactly Confucius means by understanding the will of Heaven.

Confucius said: "I do not blame Heaven, nor do I blame Man. In my studies, I start from below and get through to what is up above. If I am understood at all, it is perhaps by Heaven" (*Analects* XIV). The scholar of classical linguistics Huang Kan interprets this as: "Starting from below is studying the affairs of Man; getting through to what is above is reaching the will of Heaven. I have made a study of the affairs of Man: the affairs of Man have good luck and bad, and therefore I do not blame Man; above is the will of Heaven; the will of Heaven can be for you or against you, and therefore I do not blame Heaven." As we can see, the key to this is the word *understand*: you must be able to come to terms with whatever fate has in store for you. When you can do this, whether it is favorable or unfavorable; when you know all the good and bad in our world, and know that all of this is in fact all very natural, then you can tackle it rationally and respond to it calmly.

"I do not blame Heaven, I do not blame man" might be words that are often said even today, but they are much easier said than done. If you can stop yourself complaining, if you can keep all your carping and criticism bound firmly in your heart, then you will become the sort of person who no longer shunts blame onto others.

This idea of keeping quiet also relates to speaking ill of others. Confucius said: "The *junzi* gets through to what is above; the petty gets through to what is down below" (*Analects* XIV). Only the petty spend all their time in malicious gossip and personal disputes. The *junzi,* on the other hand, pays more attention to the inner heart, building a set of convictions for himself and pursuing his destiny. Confucius said: "A man has no way of becoming a *junzi* unless he understands Destiny; he has no way of taking his stand unless he understands the rites; he has no way of judging men unless he understands words" (*Analects* XX).

He believed that the perfection of a person's inner heart, and their desire to conform to their destiny, were so much more important than imposing their demands on society or making people behave in a particular way.

For Confucius, the three stages of life—"understanding

destiny," "understanding the rites of society," and "understanding words"—occur in reverse order. First, we learn words and we come to understand other people and the society we live in through talking to one another and reading books; but understanding words alone is not enough for you to find your feet in society. But we also need to understand ceremony and ritual, all of the things that enable you to respect others. A little more respect will leave you with fewer complaints. The highest level is understanding destiny. To understand destiny is to become a *junzi,* Confucius's ideal, at which point we will have created a self-contained system of values for ourselves, our inner heart will be suffused with a calm, matter-of-fact strength, and we can use this strength in all our interactions with the external world.

Knowing the will of heaven means that at fifty you will have an inner firmness of purpose. You will have achieved the state of "not blaming Heaven and not blaming Man": you will remain unswayed by external things.

The ancient philosopher Zhuangzi has a very similar outlook: "When all the world flattered him it did not make him increase his efforts; when the whole world condemned him it did not make him downhearted. He drew a clear line between what was inside and what was outside, and understood the difference between true glory and disgrace, but he stopped here."

In other words, when all the world is praising you, you will not react to this praise and, equally, when all around you are finding fault with you and saying that you have done wrong, you will not lose heart, but will persist, unwavering, in the beliefs you have fixed upon. This is what is meant by "drawing a clear line between what is inside and what is outside," and understanding "glory" and "disgrace."

What we call growing and maturing is a process by which the inner heart gradually becomes stronger through experience, and we acquire the ability to take external things and transform them into inner strength.

The state of "understanding the will of Heaven," is something we in China tend to naturally associate with the kung-fu novels of Jin Yong.

Knowing the will of heaven is a kind of fixity of purpose, and we can use this fixity of purpose to deal with the outside world.

In Chinese martial arts novels, when a young swordsman first appears on the scene, he generally wields a precious sword of incomparable sharpness, without equal throughout the land, and makes a splendid show with his whistling blade and balletic, graceful bearing. But by the time he has improved his martial skills through dedication and practice, has truly settled down to the life of a swordsman, and become a fighter of some little fame, the sword he uses may just be a blunt blade that he has never bothered to sharpen. By this stage, however, sharpness no longer matters to him, as his inner wisdom and experience have become richer and more solid. And by the time this man has become a famous master swordsman, and his skills have overcome all the champions the other schools had sent to defeat him, he may have no sword at all, just a stick. To him, the sharpness and quality of the metal are no longer important; anything he cares to pick up will do. By the time he has attained the highest state of all—the state of Dugu Qiubai, the hero who sought endlessly for an opponent who could match him in battle—he carries no weapon at all: all his martial arts skills have been subsumed into his heart and mind through years of deep study, and he can create the essence of a sword by just stretching out his hands. By this time his enemies have no strategies or tricks to match him, because he has already reached the state where he needs none. Since he fights without strategies or tricks, his opponent is left baffled, unable to work out what he has done, and powerless to defeat him.

In Chinese culture the highest state that any person can reach is that of mastery. What Confucius called "knowing the will of Heaven" is achieved through years of deep study and practice, absorbing all kinds of truths and through them finally achieving harmony and self-elevation. And only then will you be ready to reach the next state.

Confucius said: "At sixty my ear was attuned." But what does this mean? As we will see, an "attuned ear" is the ability to listen to any words, no matter what kind of words they are, and when looking at any issue, to always take the point of view of the person who spoke the words.

However, in real life, we often meet with things that don't go the way we would wish, and hear things that are not pleasant to hear. How can we really achieve an attuned ear?

Once you have a thorough understanding of the will of heaven, and a great inner strength of purpose, you will reach the state that Confucius described as having an attuned ear. You will have attained the greatest possible ability to respect others, you can understand the argument behind any issue, you can listen to all kinds of voices with an open mind, and you can put yourself in other people's shoes to understand why they say the things they do.

Attuning the ear is a sympathy for the world and all the people in it, that is, understanding and tolerance.

There is a common Chinese expression that describes this and it roughly translates as "grieve for the world and pity the people." In other words, by knowing everyone's motives and desires, you will achieve greater understanding and tolerance.

When we see other people's ways of life through our own value system, we may be shocked; but if we know what brought that person to the place where they are today, then perhaps we can be a bit more understanding.

There is an old saying: Two clouds can only come together to produce rain when they meet at the same height.

So who are the people who have attuned their ears? They are those who, whether their cloud is five thousand or five hundred yards high, are always aware of where the other person's is. This is the way in which Confucius dealt with all his different students, fitting each lesson to suit the pupil.

Those who want to achieve an attuned ear must make themselves infinitely open and expansive; be able to meet with minds at many different heights; not stick to their own unvarying standards and stubbornly remain at the same height, like the man in the folktale who dropped his sword from his boat and made a notch on the side so he could fish the sword out once he got to the shore, or the man in another folktale who, having once managed to catch a rabbit that ran into a tree and stunned itself, spent days sitting by the same tree, waiting for another rabbit to come along.

After taking in all knowledge, and being forged in the refiner's fire, all our study and hard work will bring us to a genuine mastery of our knowledge.

It's just like a common school physics experiment, where the teacher hands out a pencil and a circle divided into seven parts, which are colored in with the seven colors of the rainbow, then pierced with the pencil and spun round at high speed to reveal the color white. A color that is created by the blending of the seven vivid colors of the rainbow.

Confucius's state of "the attuned ear" is the fusion of the rules of the external world within our inner heart. Only once you have this coming together as a foundation for all the rest, can you reach the highest Confucian state.

Confucius said: "At seventy I followed my heart's desire without overstepping the line." What does this mean? When all rules and high principles have become habits of life, you will be able to successfully follow your heart's desire. This is the highest state that any individual can aim at. But although such a state as this seems to be easy and accessible, a person must first be tempered by a thousand blows of the hammer before he or she can reach this state.

I once read the following story:

There was once an image of the Buddha in a temple. This statue was exquisitely carved from granite, and every day many people came to pray in front of it. The steps leading up to this Buddha were cut from the same granite from which the statue had been taken.

Finally one day these steps became discontented and raised a protest, saying: "We started out as brothers; we both came from the body of the same mountain. What gives them the right to trample on us but bow down to you? What's so great about you?"

The Buddha statue said calmly to them: "That's because it only took four blows of the knife to make you what you are today, but I had to suffer ten thousand cuts and blows before I could become a Buddha."

Looking at the state of human life that Confucius described, the further through life we get, the more he emphasizes the inner heart, and the more calm and relaxed we should become, but before you can reach this state of calm, you must be forged and remade hundreds and thousands of times.

We should view the progression of human life from fifteen to seventy that Confucius described as like a mirror held up to us, in which we can examine ourselves at different stages in our lives. Through it we will be able to see whether our own spirit has taken its stand, whether we have started to lose some of our doubts, whether we are starting to take in the great truths of the world, whether we can show understanding and compassion toward others' failings, and whether we have managed to follow our heart's desire. If, at twenty or thirty, we can reach, ahead of schedule, the state we should be in at forty and fifty and have already built up a clear and lucid system of values, and are already able to transform the pressures of our society into a flexible strength that will allow us to bounce back, and if we are able to achieve a kind of calm, steady pursuit of our heart's desire without overstepping the line . . . then we can safely say that we have lived a truly meaningful life.

Scientists once performed the following experiment:

In order to obtain an exact measurement of endurance of the common pumpkin, they placed weights on a group of pumpkins, at the very limit of what each could bear.

All the different pumpkins were supporting different weights, but one particular pumpkin was under the most pressure. From a few grams one day to tens of grams the next, to hundreds of grams, and finally to kilograms, by the time this pumpkin had matured, it had a weight of several hundred kilograms pressing down on it.

At the end of the experiment the scientists cut open the pumpkin and its fellows, to see if there was anything unusual about them.

Other pumpkins opened easily at the first blow of the knife, but knives bounced right off this pumpkin, and in the end they had to hack it open using a chainsaw. Its flesh was as tough as the wood of a mature tree!

What experiment is this? It is an experiment of life, a portrait of us all in the modern environment in which we live, and of the flexible strength of our hearts.

Only by building up a system of values for the heart can we change pressure into flexibility and spring back.

Faced with competition and pressure like today's, what reason do we have not to become mature ahead of time? The words of Chairman Mao's poem, "Seize every moment, for ten thousand years are too long," could not be more appropriate today. If ten thousand years are too long, so, too, are seventy.

The study of *The Analects of Confucius,* of any of the great classics, and of all the experiences of the ancient sages and wise men, ultimately has only one, essential purpose: to make our lives more meaningful under the radiance of their wisdom, to shorten the road we have to travel, to make us start to feel and think as early as possible like a *junzi,* full of benevolence and kindness, to be able to live up to the *junzi*'s standards of social justice, and to be able to stand up with pride and give a good account of our inner hearts and our professional and social duties.

I believe that the most important thing about the sages is the way in which they describe the great journey of human life in simple language, and the way their children, grandchildren, and remote descendants put it into practice, generation after generation, whether in ignorance or with intent, painfully or joyfully. In this way, the soul of a nation was formed.

Wherever we are we can let the spiritual power of the ancient classics combine with our contemporary laws and rules, fusing seamlessly together to become an essential component of our lives, to let every one of us build for ourselves a truly worthwhile life. This is surely the ultimate significance of Confucius in our lives today.

TRANSLATOR'S NOTE

When I first read through the Chinese text of what was to become *Confucius from the Heart*, I was pleasantly surprised at what an easy task I appeared to have in front of me. Although it was based on the works of a thinker who has been dead for more than 2,000 years, the book was straightforward and wonderfully easy to follow. Yu Dan has a remarkable ability to make the complex and many-layered issues she writes about appear as something delightfully straightforward and easy to understand.

Bringing this clarity and accessibility into English, however, had it challenges. Chinese and English are two very different languages. There are many aspects of the Chinese language that do not have a one-to-one match in English. The way in which the Chinese language approaches time and tenses, for example, is quite different from the way English goes about it. Words often do not have an exact equivalent; rather, I would have to choose between two or three words that are *almost* the same.

One word that you will often see in this text is the term 君子,

pronounced *junzi*, a classical Chinese term often translated as "gentleman" or "the whole man." The concept of *junzi* and the whole meaning and full implications of this word cannot be expressed in one word in English. Nonetheless, it is a vital, key term in this book, and many of Yu Dan's most interesting remarks on ideal human behavior revolve about this word. "Gentleman" doesn't convey the real meaning of *junzi,* and "the whole man" will not do, either. Unlike in Confucius's time, when women generally were not educated and never were considered as rational beings independent of their menfolk, in Yu Dan's world men and women alike can aspire to become *junzi*. In the end I decided to keep the Chinese word for this uniquely Chinese concept and simply say *junzi*.

The Chinese original of this book is easy to follow and has been intentionally made so by using a relatively small number of Chinese characters, ingeniously combined to form understandable concepts. My intention was to replicate the same experience with the English translation. I luckily had the opportunity to speak both to Yu Dan and her Chinese editors at Zhonghua Book Company, who kindly answered all my questions, and there were a great many of them. Understanding the definition of a word in Chinese was sometimes only the first step toward translating it. Of the four words for "self-cultivation" used in this book, what exactly are the differences between them, and how important were they? What about the two different (but plainly not interchangeable) words used for "ambition"? When Confucius spoke about "all under Heaven," did he mean the whole world, or just China? What about when Yu Dan uses the term? A good example of this is the word **淡定**, which Yu Dan uses to describe a state of mind that can help us find peace and our proper place in the world, and which was explained to me as a combination of "peaceful," "stable," and "ordinary and even a bit dull." With this word, I usually had to use one or two of the concepts above, combined in different ways depending on the context.

This book will also give western readers the opportunity to learn about important facts of Chinese tradition. Yu Dan talks about Tao Yuanming, a deservedly famous poet in China but not well known worldwide. Another example is the creation myth of Pan Gu: all Chinese have heard this story, but to westerners, the "cosmic egg" with Pan Gu in the middle of it is hard to imagine. However, I managed to provide a description that was neither too pedantic nor too unclear. For the same reason, the phrase "as we all know" sometimes ended up reading "as everyone in China knows." I expanded slightly on Yu Dan's original words to make sure that readers knew enough of the background to follow what was being said.

So if translating this book was not easy, why bother to translate it at all? The reason is that this book, a highly influential bestseller in China, contains ideas that are of importance to anybody who is living in a time of change and insecurity, and longs for stability.

At present, China is going through a period of profound change, which has brought to its people both exciting challenges and a sense of deep unease. Most Chinese people are now much better off materially than they were twenty years ago, but the price of this has been a growing uncertainty, as the old ideals and convictions have been steadily undermined and social isolation has increased. Many people have started to look to traditional ideas and culture to find answers to their problems, and it is this large and growing group who have found in Yu Dan's book some of the answers they are looking for.

This is not a scholarly interpretation of the classics, but a very personal reading of them through the eyes of a highly intelligent modern woman who is sharing some of the things she has learned from *The Analects of Confucius:*

How can we deal with life when things are not going our way?
How can we choose our friends wisely?
How can I make myself a better person?

All these questions are as close to the hearts of western readers as they are to the hearts of the Chinese. That is why there are things in this book for every reader to find and treasure.

As the famous Chinese TV personality and popular culture expert Yi Zhongtian says in his introduction to the first edition of this book: "I do not know if this is the Confucius of the scholars, I do not know if he is the Confucius of history, and I do not know if this is the true Confucius. But I do know that this is our Confucius, a people's Confucius, an eternal Confucius. We need this Confucius, and we welcome him."

Printed in the United States
By Bookmasters